MoMS
Go Where Angels
Fear to Tread

MoMS

Go Where Angels Fear to Tread

Adventures in Motherhood

Joan Wester Anderson

Guideposts
New York, New York

Moms Go Where Angels Fear to Tread

ISBN-13: 978-0-8249-4781-1

Published by Guideposts
16 East 34th Street
New York, New York 10016
www.guideposts.com

Distributed by Ideals Publications, a division of Guideposts
2636 Elm Hill Pike, Suite 120
Nashville, Tennessee 37214

Guideposts and *Ideals* are registered trademarks of Guideposts.

Acknowledgments

Material in this book previously appeared in the magazine *Marriage and Family Living* published by Abbey Press.

Scripture quotations marked (NAB) are taken from the *New American Bible*, published by Thomas Nelson Publishers. Copyright © Catholic Publishers, Inc., 1971, a division of Thomas Nelson, Inc. All rights reserved.

Scripture quotations marked (NIV) are taken from *The Holy Bible, New International Version.* Copyright © 1973, 1978, 1984 International Bible Society. Used by permission of Zondervan Bible Publishers.

Scripture quotations marked (RSV) are taken from the *Revised Standard Version of the Bible.* Copyright © 1946, 1952, 1971 by Division of Christian Education of the National Council of Churches of Christ in the U.S.A. Used by permission.

Library of Congress Cataloging-in-Publication Data

Anderson, Joan Wester.
  Moms go where angels fear to tread : adventures in motherhood / by Joan Wester Anderson.
      p. cm.
  ISBN 978-0-8249-4781-1
  1. Motherhood. 2. Motherhood—Humor. I. Title.
  HQ759.A483 2009
  242'.6431—dc22
                                         2008055559

Cover design by Kathleen Lynch
Cover photograph of mop by Corbis
Cover photograph of background by Getty Images
Interior design by Lorie Pagnozzi
Typeset by Nancy Tardi

Printed and bound in the United States of America

10 9 8 7 6 5 4 3 2 1

For Kelly, Sean, Jack and Michael,
who are moving the story along . . .

Contents

Introduction

Hello, friend. I guess you might say, if anyone asked, that you know me as a writer of goose-bumpy angel and miracle stories. But first and foremost, I am a faith-filled (although often bewildered and exhausted) mom—someone probably just like you—who muddles through each day hoping that God hasn't forgotten me. And He hasn't. We seem to get along well, and He ultimately sends me what I need. In fact, one marvelous and mysterious night, He sent me an angel.

It came about because my son Tim, usually intelligent, decided to drive from New England with a few friends to celebrate Christmas with us in the Chicago area. This would have been fine, except that the entire Midwest was shivering under an unprecedented cold snap. When I pointed out on the phone that temperatures of thirty-five degrees below zero—not the wind chill, the actual temperature—were expected, Tim sighed and accused me of being overly protective. And so the boys came, chugging through the Pocono Mountains, almost driving off the road in Ohio whiteouts and finally losing their way in the middle of the night in an Indiana cornfield. And yes, by then the temperature *was* thirty-five degrees. Below.

One state away, I was praying for them. And was it my prayers or theirs that suddenly summoned a tow truck driver to the very road they were stranded upon? An ordinary-looking trucker, a man of few words who explained nothing but hitched them to his vehicle and found help for them? A fellow who, by the time they thought to ask him for the bill, had disappeared, leaving no tracks in the snow? We never found him, but I began to wonder if there were angels watching over every family, just waiting to be asked to pull their share of the load.

For as experts remind us frequently, a woman's days are filled with stress. It's part of our job description as we care for spouse, kids, elderly parents, grandchildren; as we show up for our jobs; as we nourish our faith and friendships through meetings and ministries (and has anyone mentioned groceries?). By default, we cope with a myriad of time stealers: Filling out forms (insurance, school, government). Cleaning out drawers, the ones that won't close anymore (maybe because they're glutted with forms). Organizing toys. Gardening. Supervising children's computer time. Helping with homework (how much help is too much?).

We are experts at waiting: For the due date, yours or another's. At the dentist's office. At the auto mechanic's. For the electrician. For your husband to get on with the basement remodeling. For the teenagers to get home from the dance. For the day—and there must be one—when we will understand the world and our place in it.

We are pros at feeling guilty too, often at the hands of well-intentioned experts. I know a competent young mother who worries about her fourteen-month-old son because he has not yet mastered the art of speaking; more specifically, he is supposed to be saying five words at this point in his development—according to the charts. He doesn't say any. Yes, her child walked at ten months, enjoys Mozart and screams with delight when he hears his daddy's key in the lock, but what do any of these accomplishments mean if Baby hasn't measured up to the standards some nameless study has set for him? From my experience, if you rely on God's help and second on your own good instincts, you'll be happier for it.

Today, the maternity clothes are a lot more stylish than they used to be. There are two-income families, better educations, wonderful vacations, amazing gadgets—but all too frequently a stay-at-home mom has no one to talk to. Days can go by (especially in inclement weather zones) when she sees no one taller than three feet. If the kids are a bit older, she spends more time carpooling each day than sleeping. Complete neighborhoods may become ghost towns by eight o'clock each morning, as the worker bees leave the hive; or perhaps she is one of them and must battle guilt and the ever-present clock as she hurries to the day care center and squeezes in a few errands before work. A woman who once worked in a research lab and attended stimulating biology lectures secretly fears that she will soon be talking baby talk. A former counselor cannot figure out why her life is so fragmented and confused, and why—although she would die for her children—she's having a hard time living for them. We've all had those moments. But as out of synch as our lives can feel, we should never underestimate our own strength.

God does send you what you need. And if an angel isn't available, Mom will go in and get the job done.

I've discovered many ways to bring balance (and sanity) back when it seems to be getting away from me—everything from joining a young mother's club at church, to working half-time until the kids are older, to admitting that this particular phase of child rearing is probably not going to be my favorite. But a three-pronged attack probably works best.

Tactic One: Take some time for yourself every day. Call an old friend or get started on a new interest. Bar the door if you must, or throw a tantrum. These are called "mental health breaks," and they are as important as breathing.

Tactic Two: Invite angels into your family. Check the Bible for some of the wondrous events angels attended in biblical times and realize that the blessings they brought to those people, they are bringing to us as well.

Tactic Three: Learn to laugh—the endorphins laughter releases are better than wine. (Well, close.) In the midst of the craziness of kids, pets, dead plants and accident-prone husbands, you'll make your home a little piece of heaven on earth.

MoMS
Go Where Angels
Fear to Tread

1   Intensive Training Course

One of my firmest beliefs is that every couple contemplating holy wedlock should be required to undergo intensive training. We have schools to teach every other skill; why not demand a minidiploma before John and Jane are permitted to register their preferences at Target and check honeymoon rates to Cancun?

Yes, there are already marriage preparation courses and computerized tests, mostly church-sponsored, and that's great. But I can't help wondering if the instructors deal mainly in theory, or if they themselves are battle-scarred veterans of the two-merging-into-one scrimmage. If I were to design a truly practical course, for example, I'd require all engaged couples to wallpaper a room together. There's nothing like a joint decorating project to really get to know one another. Couples would pick out the paper (looking through a minimum of twenty-five sample books), measure the room (one with plenty of windows and uneven crevices), calculate the cost, faint, look through another twenty-five books, consider using only border paper, order the paper, back-order the paper, phone the manufacturer about the paper, assemble tools, mix paste, spill paste, cut, weep, reorder. . . . Well, you get the idea.

Follow-up classes might include arranging furniture together, hanging pictures together, or for a change of pace, hosting a dinner party for both sets of in-laws together. Couples who are still dewy-eyed after these encounters should probably *teach* the next session—they've obviously got something special.

Another session would involve sick husbands. When a husband contracts a cold, flu or other death-defying disease, he's a changed creature from the stalwart male with whom she recently exchanged "in sickness and in health" vows. Saying he reverts to childhood is less than accurate. What child would turn pale at the sight of a cough drop? No, the ailing husband is rarely dealt with in depth, yet his bewildered bride needs much advice during this crisis.

She should know that, depending on his temperament, a man will react to a sore shoulder or the sniffles by (a) blaming her and being surly, (b) convincing himself it's the plague, making out his will and being surly or (c) pretending he feels fine, carrying on as usual, developing pneumonia, blaming her and being surly. All three types will require special menus, including foods that previously elicited no interest, a pyramid of tissue boxes (yes, even for a pulled muscle), frequent servings of lemonade and plenty of reassurance—especially since he insisted *she* phone the doctor and now demands to know why she didn't ask the following questions: "Is it contagious? Is it terminal? Where did you get your medical degree?"

Her strongest ally here is time. Soon, Husband will emerge

from the Valley of the Shadows and bounce off to work, while suggesting that in the future she not get so overwrought about illness.

My ideal marriage course would also include a seminar on finances. How will he deal with the fact that his fiscally conservative wife has not yet discovered that one can take money *out* of a savings account? How will she cope with a mate so addicted to the sound of ringing cash registers that he cannot mow the lawn without taking his Visa card along? Engaged pairs would learn that whoever handles the money worries about the money; the other partner gallops through life yelling, "Charge!" And unless bankruptcy is a distinct possibility, the twain rarely meet. Nor should they, since one of the pair can't rest until the checking account has been balanced, while the other figures that if the total looks reasonable, why fret?

"How much was the check for on the twenty-ninth?" Wife asks Husband.

"The twenty-ninth? Let's see ... what was the amount?"

"That's what I'm asking. Who was it to and for how much?"

"*Hmm.* Was that the week the tire blew? Or wait a minute —weren't we celebrating our anniversary that night?"

"Our anniversary's next month."

"Oh. Actually I must have been thinking of your birthday." The room temperature has suddenly dropped forty degrees.

"That's in August!" Slammed door. Unbalanced checkbook.

There should be at least one class devoted to timing—that little detail that wreaks havoc on even the most devoted duo, especially when Punctual Patty links up with Late Lester—and they usually do. My husband's idea of being on time is loosely translated as "arriving before anyone is saying good-bye." And there's the matter of inner clocks: When we were dating, neither of us noticed that he was a night owl and I was an early bird. After our "I do's," I realized that waking him involved four alarm clocks and, occasionally, a tap-dance routine on his chest. At parties, however, I'd prop my eyes open with one hand and give him desperate "let's go home!" signals with the other, which he always ignored.

"What kind of a man has never in his whole life seen a sunrise?" I once shrieked in frustration.

"What kind of woman spends a night out exchanging tuna recipes and dozes off during the Super Bowl?" he countered.

Over the years we have adjusted. He's now the early riser and makes the best coffee in the neighborhood. But wouldn't it be nicer if we had been forewarned?

And what of belongings, especially when one partner is a casual sort and the other goes quietly berserk at the drop of a dust mote? It's not long after the honeymoon when his socks tossed in the middle of the coffee table, his wet towels on the bedroom carpet, or his closet stuffed with high school sports gear plunge her into cardiac arrest. Or her compulsive attachment to the vacuum cleaner and her collection of aerosol cans send him out searching for an all-night poker party. Hammering out a compromise can take months of rereading the marriage vows, looking for loopholes.

Finally, couples in my ideal marriage class would be willing, nay eager, to make God the center of their lives. He certainly is primary in this labor of love and is only waiting to be asked to pull His share of the load. There would be evening prayer, of course—a quiet time when husband and wife join hands and ask for guidance and forgiveness. But couples would also learn the fine art of brevity in heavenly sharing. There are very few family situations that "Help, Lord! Right now!" won't cover. And it beats talking to yourself. God can also touch you gently with hope (and a reminder that love is not a feeling, but a commitment).

Marriage class would emphasize that similar backgrounds and values are important because they provide a firm foundation on which a couple can build. But differences in tastes, temperaments and opinions, while perilous, can also add spice to a shared life. A Republican can coexist with a Democrat, Arlene Athlete can merge happily with Sedentary Sam, and a red-and-orange personality can thoroughly enjoy a blue-green mate. All it takes is compromise, honesty, give-and-take, patience and plenty of love.

And perhaps a course to explain it all.

"For I know well the plans I have in mind for you," says the Lord,
"plans for your welfare, not for woe. Plans to give you a future
full of hope. When you call me, when you go to pray to me,
I will listen to you. When you look for me, you will find me.
Yes, when you seek me with all your heart, you will find me
with you," says the Lord, "and I will change your lot. . . ."

—JEREMIAH 29:11–14 (NAB)

2 What's in a Name?

After the result of the ultrasound has been joyfully announced to the immediate world, and the expectant couple has stocked up on disposable diapers and started a college fund, there's only one issue left: what shall we name the baby?

This is an important decision. According to experts, an individual's name can have a strong influence on his or her personality development. Nothing like adding a little more stress to the situation, right? One university study found that students named Bertha or Albert scored lower on achievement tests than did peers with more updated monikers such as Matt or Caroline. Abraham, Herbert and Ike all got elected to the highest office in the land, but would you really want to take the chance?

Help, of course, is available. Obstetricians scatter little what-to-name-the-baby booklets around their waiting rooms, and grandparents-to-be hint broadly that Aunt Ethel or Uncle Egbert would be thrilled with a namesake (so would Gram and Gramps, but they don't want to act too pushy).

Your tennis partner probably has an opinion on the matter. So do the neighbors, your coworkers and any stranger on the street. Whom should you listen to? How can you make up your mind?

Take it from an old pro: It isn't an easy decision. But you might want to consider some of the following points as you move toward that birth certificate moment.

Rule One: Steer clear of weird names, the ones you're going to have to constantly explain. According to one of my references, Pippa means "lover of horses" and Ahern means "horse lord." These qualities are probably helpful, especially if you live on a ranch. But imagine yourself explaining Pippa to the pediatrician, crossing guard, Brownie leader, volleyball coach and the high school guidance counselor, whose services both you and Pippa are probably going to need if this keeps up. There has to be a better way to get through life.

Rule Two: Avoid peculiar spellings for the same reason. Siobhan or Allyssha may look impressive on a birth announcement, but think of all the teachers who are going to mispronounce your darling's name during roll call.

Rule Three: Consider how the name will wear. It may be delightful when your offspring is a tyke, but a bit ridiculous by the time she goes on Medicare. (By the 2030s, I suspect we're going to have a lot of Grandma Ashleys around.) On the other hand, just because you want your son to grow up to be a tycoon is no reason to go overboard: Newton, Farthington and Wolcott may be impressive titles, but not when a nine-pounder is wearing one of them. Of course, you can get around this by choosing a name that can be shortened depending on personality or age: Libby, Liz or Betsy for

Elizabeth; Tim, Timmy or TJ for Timothy John. A good way to judge durability is to stand at an open window and yell the name into the sunset. (You'll be doing that frequently as Baby explores the neighborhood, so it's wise to get in shape.)

Rule Four: Think about your infant's heavenly sponsors. Although some saints have interesting names (how about Dymphna or Chrysostom?), you should know that children may take on the characteristics of their patrons. Are you prepared? Do you want your own Raphael (angel of travelers) navigating unfamiliar neighborhoods as a preschooler or hitchhiking across the country? Do you want Elizabeth (patron of hospitality) inviting twenty teenage girls to a sleepover every weekend? Will you be able to provide bed and board to the stray cats, wounded birds and pregnant chipmunks that Francis (patron saint of animals) drags home? Can you tolerate the how-comes, whys and buts of your own (doubting) Thomas?

Rule Five: Don't start a tradition by planning to give all your babies names that begin with the same letter. I once roomed with a mother who had done just that and was quietly desperate at the thought of coming up with yet another choice. "It seemed like such a unique idea at the time," she sobbed into her bed jacket. "First Jimmy, then John, then Jeffrey and Joe. How were we to know they'd all be boys, all nine of them?" Judson was a truly adorable infant, and by the time my roommate went home, she was resigned to it all. But I was secretly glad that I hadn't been that clever.

Rule Six: You might also figure how your baby's name is going to blend with the rest of the family's titles. Jim is a nice name, but not a good idea if he has siblings named Ken or

Dan or Kim. Telephone messages can get confusing. So can mail if you have senior and junior members of the household or if your son's name is Patrick and yours is Patricia. Of course this system works well if you're trying to avoid bill collectors and irate neighbors. And how does the name blend with your surname? Jeffrey is a popular choice but not if his last name is going to be Jefferson. Nor will Neil harmonize with Beale.

Rule Seven: Finally, tread carefully when reflecting on neutral names like Jamey, Robin or Leslie. You can always emphasize the masculine or feminine side via a special spelling (Tracie instead of Tracy), but now we're back to Rule Number One.

The name game can be challenging, but it's really academic. As any new parent can testify, a baby is soon called the baby, Sweetheart, Precious and Mommy's little honey in addition to his or her more formal title. By the time the child is ten or twelve, a summons like "hey, you" or the smell of pizza will bring them running.

So take the plunge, make your choice and don't worry. Someday *your* baby will be naming *his* baby—and guess who'll have the last laugh?

> "I have called you by name, you are mine."
>
> —ISAIAH 43:1 (RSV)

3 First, Second or Third

I went to a niece's baby shower yesterday and was intrigued by all the delightful gizmos that have popped onto the market since my own brood was potty trained. But one thing hasn't changed: There always seems to be a marked difference among the first, second and third baby in any family.

With our first—and I suspect we were typical—emphasis was on preparation. We took Lamaze, pored over Dr. Spock and lost sleep worrying about the proper kindergarten experience. Knowing that Baby couldn't possibly enter this world without a host of essential equipment, we re-mortgaged the house to purchase the required French provincial crib and canopy, complete with color-coordinated linens. (Bright primary colors stimulate an infant's intelligence, we had been informed, and the design on the sheets could determine whether our child was accepted into the college of his choice.) We bought something for Baby to lie down in, something to sit up in, something to lean on. (One item accomplished all three functions, and diced vegetables at the same time.) We bought a set of Baby Einstein videos, stocked up on surgical gowns and masks and, after the Blessed Event, stationed a Board of Health representative at the front door to require two character references from visitors bold enough to request a viewing.

"Becoming a proper parent is exhausting," Husband remarked one morning, bleary-eyed after taking all-night guard duty at the side of Baby's crib. "Do you think we're overdoing it just a bit?"

"Certainly not." I tested the bathwater with a digital thermometer while setting the radio to a Spanish station so Baby's bilingual education could begin. "He's worth it, isn't he?" He was, indeed.

Subtle changes began, however, with Arrival Number Two. Since the eldest had not yet outgrown his French provincial bed and the crammed nursery couldn't accommodate a second, we set up a portable crib in the corner of Husband's closet and deposited Precious Princess inside. She cuddled into her nest, happily sucking on the shirt sleeves that dangled over her. One night I forgot to set the alarm clock for her nutritionally necessary 2:00 AM feeding; she surprised us all by sleeping until dawn.

By this time, we had dismissed the Board of Health employee, so I guarded against germs with a brisk morning vacuum and another in the afternoon, avoiding friends whose children had runny noses, which included just about everyone I knew. Princess thrived. I scrapped the toddler swim class and played nursery rhymes on my harmonica. Princess bounced and squealed. I fed her out of warmed baby-food jars—her brother had long since broken the heat-controlled feeding dish—and during her occasional crying jags, I held her over one shoulder while doing the newspaper crossword puzzle. The jags never seemed to last very long.

"Obviously a different sort of temperament," Husband remarked, observing Precious one morning as she contentedly banged two pot lids together. "Or have we changed?"

"Certainly not!" I poured some water into the kitchen sink and gave our daughter a sponge to play with as I dunked her. "She's worth it, isn't she?" She certainly was.

Baby Number Three put in an unexpectedly early appearance, two weeks before his due date; I was engrossed in a television drama and barely made it to the hospital in time. Princess now occupied the French provincial crib, which had lost a wheel and most of its canopy, so we bedded our new infant in an empty dresser drawer lined with towels and positioned it on the dining room table—hopefully away from small prying hands. The first night home, Thirdborn screamed from 2:00 AM to 6:00 AM say the neighbors, but we apparently slept right through it.

We noticed right away that Third was the casual type. He enjoyed wearing thrift-shop sweatshirts and ate anything available that didn't move, including crumbs from the unswept floors and the covers on all the encyclopedias. He preferred to ride in the back of the wagon next to the dog on our infrequent strolls and rarely complained when visiting the hospital emergency room for an occasional stitch or three.

"A very hardy type," Husband observed one morning as Thirdborn nimbly scaled the dining room hutch. "Or have we become blasé about it all?"

"Certainly not." I tossed a bar of soap into the wading pool and went to undress Third. "We're just a little shell-shocked. But the kids are certainly worth it, aren't they?"

Whatever the position in the family, they certainly are.

> Your children are not your children.
>
> They come through you but not from you.
>
> And though they are with you yet they belong not to you.
>
> —KAHLIL GIBRAN (1883–1931)
>
> *THE PROPHET*

4   A Handy Real Estate Guide

I t happens to couples all the time. The apartment that looked so spacious when you first moved in shrinks dramatically as you acquire more furniture, gadgets, a second car and ... oh yes, children—who also tend to acquire stuff. Most people move to a condo, gaining perhaps another bedroom and maybe a bigger kitchen. It works for a while but for many of us, the day comes when it's time to buy a house.

"What could be simpler?" Husband asked as he perused the real estate section on our first morning as Lookers. "Interest rates are down, the market's booming. All we need to do is circle a few of these open houses, visit the places and see what's available. Here, this sounds nice: 'Overlooks picturesque ravine, neutrally decorated.'"

"Just what I had in mind," I agreed, imagining the kids tiring themselves out by climbing up and down the cliff.

Gram and Grandpa watched the offspring while we were gone, but the outing was short-lived. "Well?" Number Three asked upon our dejected return. "What was the house like?"

"The ravine was actually the city dump," I explained, "and every room was painted bilious beige. Other than that, it was a real bargain."

"We just have to read these ads a little more carefully," Husband pointed out. "Tomorrow we'll check the one that's 'convenient to schools, shopping centers and transportation.'"

We did. Its back door opened onto the interstate.

The following week, I took charge of our search, with the same unfortunate results. A dwelling with strong points such as "Victorian charm and country kitchen" turned out to feature a hand pump, a tub on legs and a wood-burning stove—no central heating, of course. "Aren't those tubs coming back in style?" Spouse wondered.

"Possibly," I answered. "But the updated ones also have showers."

An "airy and bright bungalow" actually had no glass in any of its windows, and part of the roof was missing. The owners had six sons—all into chemistry, baseball and hand grenades.

"What do you think we're doing wrong?" I asked my mentors, the bridge club.

"You have to learn to translate the terms used in the ads," explained Margo, a veteran of many moves and, one would expect, many ads. "Real estate writers speak a language all their own. For instance, never buy a house that has 'lots of potential.' That means nothing's been replaced or fixed in twenty years."

"If it says 'sump pump,' that means the basement floods," Ann added helpfully (her husband's been transferred five times in the past five years).

"If it says 'lake rights,' the basement *and* the backyard flood," added Flo. I'd always wondered why she had taught her children to swim before they could walk.

"And if it 'overlooks the park,' pass it up," Margo continued. "Otherwise, picnickers and day-camp kids will expect to use your bathroom."

This was fascinating. "There's actually a code?" I asked. "Then what does 'secluded area' mean?"

"Snowed in from October to April," Flo translated. I'd always wondered why she owned *two* snowblowers.

"And how about 'terms negotiable'?"

"The owner is desperate to unload it before the second floor collapses," said Ann. "And don't look at anything that's called 'spacious'; it's probably a huge old barn that costs a fortune to heat and requires a full-time cleaning crew."

"And if the house is described as 'custom,' that means it's got a weird floor plan," added Margo, reaching for the chips.

"Wow."

I told Husband about the bridge club's summation of the situation. He didn't believe me at first, but as the weeks wore on, he had to admit they were on to something. "I looked at something today that was in a 'wooded area,'" he announced glumly one evening when he came in from work.

"You probably had to carry an axe just to get from the house to the garage," I surmised.

"You're getting pretty good at this. How would you interpret 'open floor plan'?"

"The seller knocked down a few walls to remodel and then ran out of money?"

"Right." He sighed. "I thought it would be easy to find a house. Was I wrong."

Weeks wore on, and our apartment seemed to get even smaller. Then one day we stopped to visit friends and noticed that a house on their block had a new For Sale sign posted in the front yard. It was a mellow, welcoming structure with willow trees dragging their skirts on the lawn and had plenty of room for deck chairs. "Don't even think about it," our friends advised. "It's a Handyman Special."

Husband looked interested. "Don't even think about it," I echoed. "Remember: plumbing, roofing, termites. And you're the kind of guy who gets confused dealing with a childproof aspirin bottle."

And yet, there was something so welcoming about it.

The owner came by that night. "The house is loaded with extras, priced for a quick sale and has a potential rec room," he told us.

"In other words: it's got a leaky hot tub, the taxes are going up and there's a big, useless crawl space under the kitchen," Husband translated. He smiled at me, and I smiled back. "We'll take it," we chorused.

It's nice when everyone speaks the same language.

> The ache for home lives in all of us,
> the safe place where we can go
> as we are and not be questioned.
>
> —MAYA ANGELOU

5   Be Careful What You Pray For

Most mothers have an active prayer life; it goes with the territory. Even if our heavenly harangues take the more casual form ("God! Help!"), at least it's a pretty regular practice. I've always considered myself an adequate communicator, able to keep up a running commentary as I scoured pots, wiped runny noses and searched for toddlers. My Father always seemed present, smiling benevolently at my ramblings, patting me on the head like a fond parent.

But as time passed and life got more crowded and complicated, I sensed that my heavenly wires often seemed crossed. I'd "ask, seek and knock," but receive answers that were not at all what I anticipated.

The confusion started shortly after we moved to the aforementioned handyman-special house. Husband belatedly had discovered that our budget would not stretch to accommodate the handyman we needed. And so, as he explained to me, one of us had to get a part-time job.

One of us. I glanced at the four-year-old, whose income potential seemed limited. Surely Husband didn't mean *me*.

We had already established that I had very few marketable skills. I had gone to college to find a husband, found one after my sophomore year and declined to finish my higher education. What would be the point? In those days, there were only a few employment avenues open to young women: we could become secretaries, nurses, teachers, starving artists or (gulp) nuns. I had no interest or aptitude for any of these choices and had opted instead to marry, have a family and live happily ever after.

Unfortunately, Husband and I had gotten married under one set of social expectations and then society changed, primarily due to the feminist movement, but also the influence of protest movements, the unresolved war in Vietnam and other upheavals that rocked our *Leave It to Beaver* world. Husbands who had never poured themselves a cup of coffee were now expected to brew it; wives who'd left their paying jobs at the altar were encouraged to finish their degrees in order to contribute to the house down payment. Positive results would eventually flow from many of these changes, but right now, Husband and I were stuck in the middle.

I thought about looking for a job. I had a better idea. I had another baby.

A severe case of denial, you'd probably say. And you'd be right. But she was awfully cute, and when she was eight months old, I wrote my first article about her. (I frequently dashed off irate letters to our local newspaper, so it seemed like a natural extension.) Lo! The article was accepted for publication, and a few weeks later, a lovely check for twenty-five dollars was in my mailbox. Twenty-five dollars in those days bought two or three buckets of high-grade paint, and the lightbulb went on above my head. I didn't *have* to fill out job applications; I had a potential job right here, however hit-or-miss. Quickly I grabbed paper and crayon and jotted another article, this one about our kitchen blackboard and the messages it held. ("Dad, some man called. Please call him back.") A few weeks later, my article was published in our local paper and delighted friends called and another check arrived—this one large enough to finish painting the dining room, which had admittedly looked a bit odd with old yellow paint on two walls and new blue paint on the others.

Those first two sales had been fortunate, because I collected sixteen rejection slips before I sold a third article. But by now I was hooked. It seemed a perfect solution to our financial difficulties, and I would be able to follow my heart and stay home with the kids as well.

Of course I had asked God about the decision. Should I attempt to add something this unreliable to a schedule that was already bursting? Unlike most people, writers are never sure when or if they will be paid. I had no training, no "connections" and very little talent. But God seemed to have no strong reservations about my burgeoning career, so I plunged ahead.

Within a few months, however, it was obvious that God had misunderstood my intentions. I had somehow become a weekly (unpaid) columnist for a local publication (mostly ads), a twice-monthly (unpaid) reporter for a religious newspaper and was putting in so much time doing publicity for our local grade school that I had no spare hours to drum up paid assignments. "Excuse me, Lord," I pointed out one day while sorting socks. "I know we decided I should write, but aren't You forgetting something? After all, the dining room drapes are worse than tacky, the kindergartner needs his tonsils yanked, and the car has a tremor even when the engine's off. How about a little cash?"

The next day's mail brought the usual assortment of bills and circulars—and a heart-stopping slim envelope from a magazine publisher. I slid out the beautiful check and peeked at the amount. Ten dollars. I could just hear the Lord's reply: "Well, you asked for a *little* cash."

Then there was the episode with the dog, the one Eight-Year-Old kept asking to add to the family. First he simply stated his request and then, as we ignored it, progressed to burying rubber bones under the living room rug and leaving a copy of *101 Dalmatians* on my bed. When I caught him trying to stuff an Irish setter into the baby's closet, I realized it was time to pass the buck.

"God," I began firmly, "You know I have nothing against dogs, provided they stay in other people's houses. Help me figure out a way to keep Eight-Year-Old happy without one."

God must have been between crises, because He went to work right away. The very next evening, Husband came home with a small box and a medium-sized glass aquarium. "They're gerbils," he explained as I viewed the furry rodents. "I thought they'd take Son's mind off the dog."

I sent a grateful prayer heavenward and gave Spouse an extra kiss. The gerbils' superior attributes were evident; they didn't need to be walked, lived on a diet of lettuce and oat cereal (just like me) and would not teethe on leather purses.

They did, however, have one major drawback, as we

discovered a few weeks later when Son awakened us by dancing in the middle of our bed. "Thirteen!" he shrieked. "I have thirteen gerbils! This is great! Dad, can you build another room on the house so I can have a breeding lab?"

I buried my head under the pillow. My prayer had been answered; Son was happy without a dog. So why did it appear that something major had been jumbled in the earth-to-heaven transmission?

Occasionally, when I mention to God that the garden looks a bit arid, and He unleashes a three-day monsoon that reduces my housebound offspring to a whining choir, I wonder where our communication has broken down. And when I pray for a child who seems a little withdrawn, and later her exhausted teacher asks if I'm slipping stimulants into her morning orange juice, I wonder where my dialogues have failed.

Yet, what better friend have I than my Maker, Who knows my needs better than I know them myself? It's true, God, I must work more on accepting Your direction with a peaceful and serene heart. How pointless to quibble, to question Your will when I know every hair on my head is numbered and protected. How much better just to love You.

And perhaps be a bit more *specific* next time.

"For my thoughts are not your thoughts, neither are your ways
my ways," declares the Lord. "As the heavens are higher than
the earth, so are my ways higher than your ways
and my thoughts than your thoughts."

—ISAIAH 55:8–9 (NIV)

6 Out to Lunch

When our children were very small, my favorite pastime was pressing my nose against the front window and gazing out upon the Great Unknown. It seemed incredible that there was still a world out there composed of trees and stores and people blithely tripping off to work, while my environment seemed limited to strained prunes and sibling rivalry. It was no wonder that I grabbed every opportunity to leave the premises. "It's my turn to take out the garbage!" I frequently challenged Husband, who wisely backed away whenever I got That Look on my face.

During those years, my breaks from the combat zone usually took place in the evening (daytime sitters were as scarce as clean laundry, and few relished the prospect of riding herd on our four under six). I took part in the church Christmas pageant, served a few stints on the school board, rang doorbells for charity runs—any activity that brought me into contact with people who had beaten the thumb-sucking habit and didn't panic if they misplaced a particular plush bunny.

Eventually, however, a strange thing happened. The kids got older. The first time I noticed was on wash day when I trekked downstairs to the apartment building laundry room only to realize that something was missing. Let's see ... basket of dirty jeans, hamper of dirty diapers (yes, diapers were once washable), detergent, superstrength stain remover, paint remover, spit-up remover, quarters for the machines, house keys, basement keys ... wait a minute. The *kids* were missing! Two in preschool and pre-preschool, the other two still napping—it was a turning point in my life.

Even though friends had warned me that life might eventually get easier, it took a while to get adjusted, to think of myself as someone who might venture forth during daytime hours without dragging along a stroller or a box of instant oatmeal. My nighttime purse, stocked with grown-up accessories and used only when freedom beckoned, gradually became my daytime purse, unencumbered by pacifiers and small crackers. Heady with delight, I began a whirlwind schedule—this week a trip to the library (Adult Fiction rather than Thomas the Tank Engine), next week a consultation with my podiatrist. But I didn't really become a member of the We've-Got-It-Made Society until a friend said, "Let's go out to lunch."

Going out to lunch, while viewed as ordinary by members of the outside workforce, can be tantalizing to someone who's spent years sharing peanut butter in the company of toddlers, TV cartoons, a hamster and sometimes a dog. I hardly knew how to react that first afternoon when five pals and I threaded our way through a dim dining room behind a man I didn't know. "Why are we following him?" I asked.

"That's a waiter," my friend Alice explained to me patiently. "He brings our food."

"We don't have to cook it ourselves?"

Alice patted my hand. "We don't even pour our own coffee. You *have* been housebound a long time, haven't you?"

"Look at those napkins!" I gasped. "Real linen! Don't they have any paper ones that say Happy Birthday from Bozo the Clown?"

"No, sweetheart." Beth leaned across the table. "And it isn't necessary to tuck a bib under my chin. I know it's difficult to get used to pantyhose in daylight, but you are in the adult world now, with life-sized people, and you can eat anything you want, and even say anything you want."

"And go to the ladies' room all by yourself," Alice added kindly.

It was too much to take in all at once—softly glowing candlelight, background mood music, rich aromas. No one in the entire room hurled a goblet to the floor in a fit of temper or stood backward on his chair while peeling a banana. Had I died and gone to heaven? The menu was an eye-opener too. "Where is the pureed squash?" I asked Beth. "The dried bologna on wheat?"

"You'll have to settle for stroganoff or shrimp salad." She grinned. "And no, there are no Teletubby feeding spoons here, hon; this is real silverware. You remember—the kind you and your husband used to have BC (Before Children)."

It was quite a change. But except for one mad moment

when I automatically reached over and cut Alice's meat, I managed to behave with suitable decorum. And listen to the delightful conversation and laughter, which—delicious food notwithstanding—was the real reason we were Out to Lunch.

It had all started several years ago, Alice explained, when her three-year-old had thrown every towel in the household into a tub of bathwater. "I kept myself together, went to the phone, dialed a sitter, then called Beth and begged her to meet me for lunch at McDonald's."

Beth's twins had visited the hospital emergency ward twice that week, so she was primed for an hour away from the battlefront. The two had met, shared tales of woe, giggled their way through two Big Macs apiece and returned home refreshed and civilized.

"Since then, a group of us has gotten together every month," Beth said. "Sometimes we go first class and sometimes it's a bucket of chicken, but the important ingredient is the shared conversation, touching base with friends and not feeling quite so isolated."

"And being pampered too," added someone. "After all, who pours you ice water at home?"

"Usually we don't even *have* ice," I admitted.

It was an excellent idea and since then, I've made a monthly luncheon date a part of my life—grabbing a quick sandwich with an employed pal, or getting a group together in the Café Swanque. Through it all, I've learned that other women's husbands aren't perfect either, that kids are always in some kind of stage, and that laughter, love and lunch can smooth out just about any bump.

And as Husband points out, it's a lot cheaper than therapy.

> A friend is one who takes you to lunch
> even if you're not tax deductible.
>
> —AUTHOR UNKNOWN

7 Thinking about Remodeling?

When Husband and I purchased our infamous Handyman Special, we decided to "take our time, and do it right." Husband purchased an impressive array of tools and several how-to books, which the kids buried in the sand, delivered for a sandbox not yet constructed. (It never was.) When I found out eventually that "taking our time" meant that Husband would spackle a crack every third Tuesday, I threw a tantrum, and we decided to start by tackling the kitchen. We didn't have the funds for a full-scale remodeling job (why else would we have purchased a house whose floors leaned a little to the left?). So we contented ourselves with papering over the orange walls and hiding those interesting floor tiles (three different patterns) with commercial carpeting. The dated sink, vintage metal cabinets and long rollout window above the stove—with its equally long curtain that frequently blew onto a lit burner and livened things up with a visit from the fire department? Well, they would all just have to wait until our ship came in.

Time passed with no ship in sight. We painted the dining room, made the children's bedrooms perky and livable— except when the children were actually in residence—gutted and rebuilt the bathroom walls and added a deck. The kitchen, however, remained in the same prehistoric state, and we learned to keep our eyes down when passing through its portals.

"Too expensive," Husband would say when I complained about not being able to see what I was peeling, stirring or washing. "Get a floodlight."

"Too expensive," I would retaliate when he argued that the window drafts were escalating our gas bills. "Get a portable heater."

"Too expensive," we both told the kids as they strained to reach cabinets mounted from the ceiling. "Get a ladder."

I have always assumed that all men have a "fix-it" gene in their DNA that enables them to repair or construct anything involving an electric drill. But, although Husband cleans gutters, paints trim and even hoses down the driveway every Thursday as a form of therapy, ask him about the inner workings of an appliance and one is answered with a blank stare. "Honey, the kitchen light fixture is shooting sparks all over the roast."

"Yeah, I noticed that."

"Well, what are you going to do about it?"

"Eat in the dining room."

Things came to a head one day. A guest tripped over the lumps in our "temporary" kitchen carpet just as a section of wallpaper fell into my fried rice. "Kitchens are expensive to remodel," I told Husband, "but six years is a long time to wait for a ship. The children ought to know what it's like to cook in a room with a faucet that works. Come to think of it, I'd like to know too."

Husband sighed. "You've made your point. Let's call a repairman."

Repairmen. Talented as they obviously are, they don't seem to function on the same wavelength as the rest of the population. The man who services (constantly) my washer and dryer is a real sweetie. We've been on a first-name basis for years and I invite his wife to all my Tupperware parties. But his concept of emergency is not the same as mine.

"A real problem there, Mrs. A?"

"The machine's walking through the house, Al. There's water and suds flying everywhere—oh gosh, it just swallowed the cat. Can you come quickly?"

"For you, sure. How about a week from Thursday?"

And when we gutted the bathroom, the most reassuring estimate came from a local contractor who murmured, "Sure, no problem" to everything I showed him.

"You can have it done by Thanksgiving?" I asked happily.

"Sure. No problem."

"Great!"

The turkey leftovers were long gone by the time I called Contractor. "What happened to our plans?"

"Oh." There was a long pause. "You meant *this* Thanksgiving?"

Now, Husband, aware of what I was thinking, sighed. "I'll talk to Bud this week about the kitchen." Bud is the neighborhood jack-of-all-trades who keeps himself in gold-plated underwear by remodeling other people's houses. He's pricey. But he's good. We were on our way!

As expected, Bud had quite a waiting list; we signed up immediately and figured that he would probably turn up sometime in May. When May arrived, however, he hadn't yet been over to measure the cabinets, and our new windows were on back order, so we settled for August. Unfortunately, August fell right in the middle of Bud's annual Alaskan cruise. The poor neighbor across the street was still waiting for him to complete her roof. So we pushed our date back to October. By that time the windows had been delivered and were propped up against our bed (the only safe place in the house), the cabinets had been discontinued and the floor tile was no longer on sale. We settled on December.

February finally arrived and so did Bud. On the first day, he completely tore apart the kitchen and the attached laundry room, tossed the sink onto the driveway and rolled the dishwasher, refrigerator, washing machine and clothes dryer in front of our furniture in the den. The contents of the shelves and cabinets of both rooms were stacked throughout the house. This made for an interesting dilemma: how was our family going to function for the duration?

Bud then remembered a prior engagement (the lady across the street?) and disappeared for a few weeks, during which time we pulled up the kitchen carpet. All the backing, however, stayed glued to the floor. I tried to convince the kids that chiseling and scraping can be fun, but they weren't buying. To make matters more interesting, I'd forgotten to warn Bud not to plug his power drill into *that* socket and he'd blown our main artery. Thus, Husband and I found ourselves alone by candlelight for the first time in ten years.

Eventually Bud returned, pounded, measured and drilled, sending a steady spray of sawdust into our beds and bathtubs each day. I learned to wash dishes in the driveway, one cup at a time, with the garden hose. Husband rigged an elaborate network of extension cords so we could brew coffee each morning, provided one of us could lift the other over the washing machine to get to the pot. Our kids hung out at their friends' houses during mealtimes, and the preschoolers lost their jackets in a pile of old drywall. Husband used my new color-coordinated dish towels for paint rags, and I discovered that the blinds I had ordered for the new windows were a foot too short.

By the time the counters, cabinets and floor were finally installed and the appliances hooked up (except for the dryer, which had to be replaced due to another section of ceiling falling on it), the thrill of "something new" had definitely dimmed.

"This too shall pass," my mother said soothingly as she patted my shoulder. "When the scuffmarks on the ceiling are painted over, and you finish papering—"

"The rest of the wallpaper's on back order." I sniffled. "They think it might come in within six months if the pattern isn't discontinued."

"It'll all work out," she promised. "And no one will ever notice that Bud forgot to tile under the stove."

"Or that the dishwasher controls are reversed." I sighed.

"Or that the ceiling fan was installed upside-down,"

Husband added. "Actually, it's a big improvement. I think we all did a great job."

I guess we did. But from the insights we gleaned from our personal fiasco, I offer this advice to others facing a major kitchen remodeling job: plan to spend twice as much as you budgeted; plan to be without water twice as long as you expected; remember that material things do not bring happiness (although they do make cooking easier) and if possible, stay in Florida until it's all over. Maybe Bud can recommend a place.

> Between keeping house and working,
> I'm probably going to live to be a hundred.
> Or maybe it will just seem that long.

—ERMA BOMBECK (1927–1996)

8 A February Prayer

Lord, make me an instrument of Your peace. Especially during February, when winter winds continue to howl, when the snowman we so blithely built in November still stands, rock-hard and frozen, when the kids, cooped up and frustrated, vent their boredom with crashes and screams.

"He stuffed my bear down the clothes chute."

"You're a wimp!"

"*Mother-r-r-r.*"

Then give me a gentle heart, a soft word and maybe the keys to the car so I can get out of this zoo for a few hours.

Lord, teach me the meaning of patience, when the weatherman excitedly forecasts another round of blizzards and sub-zero temperatures (and I suspect my husband is hoping he'll be snowed in at the office rather than here), when the kids open the refrigerator eighty-seven times in one hour, when the nonstop sound of chewing and rattling bags fills the air, when the furnace breaks and the repairman will be out as soon as possible, which means just before Memorial Day.

Then give me a casual attitude, a faithful outlook and maybe a good novel that I can read while hiding on the top bunk.

Lord, remind me of my obligation to care for the less fortunate. When the flu bug strikes, and my bouncy tribe is reduced to wan and listless strangers, when I must locate a plastic bucket for each of them, run upstairs and downstairs with beef tea, crackers and Popsicles (and we're out of Popsicles), when telephone conversations with the pharmacist become my only link to the outside world and when my husband (the coward) has indeed been snowed in at the office.

Then remind me that this is but a brief detour in Your ongoing blessings of good health. Make me a cheerful servant, grateful that our children will recover when so many other little ones will not.

Lord, let me appreciate Valentine's Day. It's supposed to be a port in our continuing winter storm, a time to pause and celebrate love. But judging from the atmosphere around here—"You took my glue! Give it back!" "Don't you DARE touch this special heart I'm making for Daddy!" "Mom, did I tell you that I'm supposed to have six dozen pink cookies at school tomorrow?"—I need a sparkly sense of fun and anticipation, a tolerant spirit ...

And maybe a five-pound box of chocolates from Husband that he and I can stash in our closet and eat at midnight when no one's up to hear the wrappers rattle.

Lord, help me figure out how to keep a weather-weary preschooler amused. She's tired of the usual games of Wash the Play Dishes in the Sink (which ought to be renamed

Flood the Kitchen), Lint Hunt (participants pick up small pieces of debris scattered throughout the house and deposit them in the nearest waste receptacle) and Find the Doggy (who's been hiding from Preschooler since she painted him orange). Give me strength for yet another round of Go Fish, keep me from turning the DVD player into a babysitter and let Grandma phone and volunteer to take Precious Princess to a Florida resort for the duration. (Could I come too?)

Lord, give me the honesty of George and Abe, our February heroes. Grant that I may not blanch and turn away from questions such as "Can I take drum lessons?" or "How come you and Daddy were yelling this morning?" or "Who's better, boys or girls?" Grant that I may find the wisdom to settle each issue as it arises. Or maybe suggest that they go ask their father.

Lord, provide me with a balanced perspective. Help me when I ask: Why should I care if the house hasn't been thoroughly cleaned since Christmas? (It's hard to vacuum around all those pails catching the leaks anyway.) Does it truly matter if the kids drop wet jackets in the hallway or cocoa hardens in the mugs under their beds? Will I be a better person if all the socks match? (Of course, Husband may be a happier person if he doesn't have to wear that red-argyle/brown-polyester combination again.) Lord, teach me that nothing here on earth is permanent, and hardly any of it will matter in ten years' time.

Lord, grant that I may not seek to hurry this time along. For You have taught us that there is a proper place and season for everything. Perhaps in our family's enforced togetherness, we are learning things about each other, growing in ways we cannot yet understand. For it is in surviving the gray and dismal days that we really appreciate the sun.

I know February must be good for something, Lord, because You made it. Now give me the strength to endure this blessing.

And let me see a crocus tomorrow. Amen.

Surely as cometh the winter, I know
There are spring violets under the snow.

—REV. R. H. NEWELL

9   When It's Time for Preschool

As mentioned previously, the thrill of Toddler's constant presence rubs a bit thin after a while—at least, in my experience—and the motherhood-is-supposed-to-be-wonderful-so-why-am-I-weeping mood can strike without warning—from the hospital delivery room all the way up to eighth grade. There's lots of professional help out there, so no one should suffer alone or in silence. However, such moods do come to us all, whether hormonal or simply the result of enduring a nine-day rainstorm. The first time for me was when I realized that the eldest, then four years old, was a head taller than most of his peers but still wore pull-up diapers and hid a pacifier among his small computer games. It happened again when I read the same storybook forty times in two days and broke out in hives; when I secretly broke a CD of "Old MacDonald Had a Farm" (and almost torched the player as well); when the preschooler asked why ducks floated and I responded, "I don't know and I don't care. Go ask your father."

Any seasoned veteran can recognize the deeper meaning of this behavior. It's "maternal burnout" at its finest, and the remedy simply involves getting away from one's Precious for a while. You can check into a rest home, buy a one-way ticket to Greenland, step up lunches with your pals to twice a month, or opt for a more serious commitment: the preschool experience. Your child might not need it, but you certainly do.

While we read much advice on toddler separation anxiety, no one seems to realize that first-time parents have some adjusting to do as well. With this in mind, you should remember the following:

✳ On that first morning, whatever you *expect* your child to do at the preschool door will be quite opposite from what he actually does. Independent Isaac, who could get happily lost at the mall for hours if you allowed it, and speaks *only* to strangers, will dissolve into a whimpering, sobbing, clinging mass as you introduce him to his teacher. Frantically you will attempt to disentangle your hair from his iron grip, while pretending that he is your neighbor's child. The other mothers will look at you with glances both pitying and superior.

Your Timid Tammy, by contrast, will leap from her seat while the car is still in motion, elbowing other kids aside to be first in line. "Aren't you going to kiss Mommy good-bye?" you'll plead, racing after this child who, until now, couldn't eat a bowl of cereal without your sitting beside her.

"NO! Go 'way! Me do it!"

The other mothers will look at you with glances both pitying and superior.

✳ Preschool teachers always smile. They do it because they are hearing-impaired, have a psychological disorder, are on some special kind of sedative or are anticipating the Woman-of-the-Year award. Teacher will never say anything nasty about your child, but if she sends you a note saying that "Avery still has some adjusting to do," it means that you should send two sets of clean underwear tomorrow.

Communication is a two-way street, so be sure to tell Teacher anything she should know about Avery's idiosyncrasies. Does he enjoy eating sand? Will he only sing "It's a Beautiful Day in the Neighborhood" while hanging from the light fixture? Help Teacher to create the proper home-away-from-home atmosphere.

✳ Comparisons between kids are taboo. This was a tough one for me. Even though I needed some free time away from Daughter (and the feeling was definitely mutual), I thought she was basically a neat kid. That is, until my Helper Day, when I encountered the class star, Wilma Wonderful. The two girls came in together; Daughter tossed her new jacket in the corner while Wilma laid hers on a table, slipped in the hanger and ran over it carefully with a battery-operated lint remover.

Wilma was one of those girls whose curls never moved. My daughter's hair always looked as if she had just run the fifty-yard dash. Actually, she usually had. While my child was still trying to identify the primary colors, Wilma painted in oils, could construct a perfect map of South America (complete with rivers drawn in blue), had made the finals in the Little Miss Caramel contest and always remembered to say "please." Her sole function in life was to be perfect at all times, thus tossing me into a "where have I failed?" funk. It didn't surprise me that Wilma's mother played the cello, made all her Christmas ornaments by hand and modeled for *Seventeen* magazine on the side.

"Your child's doing very well in class," Teacher told me kindly on my Helper Day as we hosed glue, paint and apple juice off the floor.

"Sure." I looked at Daughter, sucking her thumb while Wilma gave the class a lecture on cooperation.

"I mean it." Teacher followed my gaze. "It isn't every three-year-old who can stay dry all morning."

"You mean ... *Wilma* ... ?" I was astonished.

"My lips are sealed."

It was hard to not look both pitying and superior as Wilma's mother arrived at the door, but I was in a hurry anyway. I was busy combing Daughter's hair before taking her to the House of Lettuce for a healthy lunch to celebrate those iron kidneys.

✦ Preschool is supposed to benefit you too. Under no circumstances should a mother use this precious free time to sew on Scout merit badges, regrout sink tiles, make committee phone calls or pick up overturned trash cans. Instead, learn to live dangerously. Shampoo and blow-dry your hair in one operation, get a library card (and then get a book), take a nap or play with the goldfish. Chores are always present, but the chance to pamper yourself at this stage of motherhood is rare.

So go to it! Enjoy yourself, enjoy the kids when they return—they'll definitely look better to you—and remember those preschool teachers in your prayers. After all, the life they're saving is yours.

> They are idols of hearts and of households;
> They are angels of God in disguise:
> His sunlight still sleeps in their tresses,
> His glory still shines in their eyes;
> Those truants from home and from heaven,—
> They have made me more manly and mild;
> And I know now how Jesus could liken
> The kingdom of God to a child.

—CHARLES MONROE DICKINSON (1842–1924)
"THE CHILDREN"

10 Pills, Drills and Me

'm not overly fond of doctors' offices—the mere mention of a blood test or even a cotton swab usually causes me to break out in a rash. Nevertheless, I've spent the majority of this week's waking hours in waiting rooms, and not by choice. Several pre-scheduled checkups—in addition to a few spontaneous visits—have filled five days with white coats and examining tables, which was novel, admittedly, but not necessarily traumatic.

No, my problems with a week like this stem not from the few seconds spent with the physician, but the lifetime one is required to spend in the physician's waiting room. A recent study concluded that patients wait there an average of thirty-two minutes, but I suspect that poll was taken in the Sahara, for I've never experienced such a whirlwind episode. Or perhaps waiting just *seems* endless when one is wedged between several tots sneezing streptococci germs on each other, a bevy of young mothers playing "Can You Top This?"—a game that requires mothers to describe gruesome childbirth pains in vivid detail—and only a stack of outdated magazines to break the monotony.

Nurses seem to take this situation in stride. Last Monday when we'd sat in the outer office for an hour and then progressed to the inner cubicles where they put you as part of their riot control program, I eventually summoned the courage to ask the nurse if it was still summer outside. She rolled her eyes apologetically. "It's *always* like this on Mondays."

On Tuesday, making a return visit with another small patient, I didn't wait to count my new gray hairs. After a mere ninety minutes, I bravely inquired as to the doctor's whereabouts. Ms. Nightingale shook her head ruefully. "It's *always* like this on Tuesdays," she confided. Thursday's nurse (another office) seemed genuinely surprised when she overheard me calling the sitter to tell her we wouldn't be home for lunch. After all, I'd only been at the office since nine, barely enough time to fill out the forms: Paternal grandmother's maiden name and food allergies? Were you recommended by (select one) a physician, a relative, a complete stranger in the checkout line? I hadn't even read the helpful literature yet ("Prunes, Bran and You"), much less had an actual exam.

I realize that one of the reasons appointment times in some offices bear little resemblance to reality is because our doctors are nice people. Because they care, they often squeeze ailing patients into an already-swollen schedule, or spend extra time with someone who's upset. And having been the recipient of such kindness, I see no reason to carp when the same care is bestowed on others. But not every case is a three-handkerchief drama right out of the afternoon soaps. And although my neighbor's solution—billing the doctor twenty-five dollars an hour waiting time—seems crass, I must admit I'm tempted.

If doctors annoy me with their terminal tardiness, how much more must our family irritate them when we finally do meet? For it is an unwritten law, at least in our domain, that the sicker a child appears (thus the more desperately urgent the appointment), the quicker his recovery—usually about five minutes before Doctor Bob, wearing jeans and a college-letter sweater under his whites, finally makes an appearance. Gone is the child's wan complexion, the fever, the unusual listlessness. "He was *very* ill," I protest as Doctor Bob, unconvinced, stares at the small body somersaulting off the examining table. Younger Brother, who, moments ago, seemed a candidate for Intensive Care, twirls merrily on the swivel chair.

"*Hmm.*" Doctor Bob sweeps one child onto his lap, peers into orifices, dodges a flying tongue depressor and looks thoughtful.

"They may be coming down with the flu," I offer helpfully in case—despite the degrees lining his walls—Doctor Bob is having a bad day. "Or perhaps a bit of bronchitis."

"*Hmm.*" He gives me a for-this-I-rearranged-my-whole-morning? glance, grabs the younger as he dashes by and subjects him to the same scrutiny. I plop Elder Brother—flushed from his romp—onto the seat beside me and give him my best "act sick!" glower.

Tension grows. Then, "A bit of bronchitis," Doctor Bob pronounces. Aha! I feel, if not vindicated, less neurotic. (Do they maintain a top secret office file, I wonder, with the dossiers on nervous mothers arranged in order of degree: Somewhat Hyper, Overly Protective, Downright Pushy, Hysteric?)

"Perhaps a touch of flu too," Doctor Bob adds, "and this boy also has ingrown toenails." It's been a bonus day.

I wish I could say the same about Nine-Year-Old's dental checkup the following afternoon. Our dentist, a master of guilt therapy, makes certain I understand that this child is headed for gingivitis—or worse—if something isn't done soon. Doctor Phyliss knows only too well that I have committed the Unpardonable Maternal Sins: (1) I've been letting the kids brush without supervision and (2) I ran out of floss last month and have been waiting for a sale.

How can I explain to this sleek, together lady that on certain days teeth, despite their acknowledged importance, rank only fourth or fifth on my priority list? They rank behind such activities as: (1) keeping the children from maiming themselves and/or each other, (2) keeping the bathroom fixtures intact (or barring that, at least fastened to the wall), and (3) keeping us from declaring bankruptcy (at least until the grade school fees are fully paid up). It's hard to interest Doctor Phyliss in my laments, however, because as she and I both know, she has our best interests at heart and is not above using scare tactics to achieve her goals.

Wearily, I drag home. At least the week is over, everyone seems healthy, and aside from the small matter of a second mortgage, the bills are paid. It's a lot to be thankful for. Quite a lot, as a matter of fact. Suddenly I picture a world without Doctor Bob, Doctor Phyliss, antibiotics, orthodontia and a thousand other blessings that help to keep us healthy and are so plentiful that sometimes, we become forgetful of the miracles.

May I be struck with a virus if I ever complain again.

Never go to a doctor whose office plants have died.

—ERMA BOMBECK (1927–1996)

11 Organization 101

Our local junior college is a lively place. In addition to the ordinary academic credits, there are plenty of special-interest classes offered, everything from Ballroom Dancing to Vegetarian Cooking to Estate Planning to Becoming a Parent. (I always thought *that* process was rather simple. Is a textbook really necessary?)

One of the most interesting catalog entries is Help! I've Got to Get Organized! The teacher is one of those perfect types that you'd love to hate but can't—she's too nice. (Even though her closets contain rows of neatly labeled garment bags and she always knows immediately what ingredient removes bloodstains from white wool carpeting.) The students, on the other hand, are somewhat bedraggled. Few have pre-registered—they never got around to it—and it's not unusual to see at least one or two women wearing mismatched socks. Several bring along their children, having forgotten to hire babysitters, which adds to the general confusion.

On our first evening, I sat next to a perky gal who proudly showed me a leather appointment book. "I decided to get off to an efficient start," she explained. "So I rummaged through the old Christmas presents in my linen closet and found this." She held it up. "Isn't it classy?"

"Sure is," I agreed. "But have you noticed the date on the front?"

She turned the book over. "2005?"

"I think we're past that year."

"Oh well,"—she shrugged—"I'll sell it at my next garage sale."

I was impressed. "I've never gotten organized enough to have a garage sale," I told her.

"Actually," she confided, "I just let people walk through the house and buy whatever they want. It beats pricing and sorting—"

"Ladies!" the teacher rapped her pencil against the desk. "Let's begin, shall we?" She beamed encouragingly at all of us and then read from a checklist. "Are you the type of woman who's afraid to open a drawer? Do you write wonderful e-mails and never hit Send? Do you have sixty-seven boxes stashed in your attic, all marked Miscellaneous? Do your children drink out of peanut butter jars and eat meals served on Tupperware lids?" We nodded.

"Then you've come to the right place," she assured us. "In this class you're going to learn how to pull the pieces of your lives together, take control of your dust and complete your Christmas shopping before December twenty-fourth!"

A murmur of disbelief swept through the room. One

woman who had forgotten to turn off her car engine headed for the parking lot. Another, wearing only one contact lens, moved closer to the overhead projector.

"The first rule of organization is to make lists," our teacher went on. "Does anyone have a list in her purse that we can use as a model?"

Several moments passed as those who had remembered to bring purses sifted through them. "Gee," my neighbor muttered, "here's that dry cleaning ticket for my husband's brown suit. I wonder what I should do now."

"Why?" I asked.

"The cleaners closed two years ago."

"I have a list," I told the teacher. "It's just an errands list, written in lip gloss on the back of a matchbook."

"Splendid," she enthused. "Please read it to us."

I did. "Pix, lv car shp, bread, cauli, p.u.Nancy dent 230, flute tun, mlk mony? Garlic, 3-rg pap, vet."

There was a long silence. "Interesting," the teacher finally observed. "Do you have any idea what it means?"

"None," I admitted. "But I think it's pretty old. We haven't owned a flute in five years."

We spent the rest of the class learning how to prepare a proper list. Since nothing in a housewife's life fits together in any logical sequence, the teacher explained, one has to keep control over the flotsam and jetsam. Hence a list of chores and errands, in order of importance, to be crossed out when completed, thus giving one a sense of achievement at the end of a day.

It worked. By midterm, I had the best-kept list on the

block. Each morning I transferred the undone chores from yesterday's list to today's, numbered them in order of urgency, checked the running grocery list on the refrigerator door, added any "must" items to the category marked "shopping," glanced through my daily appointment log and transferred all pit stops onto the master list under "errands," then tallied and included necessary phone calls, e-mails to be sent and pencils to be sharpened. There was just one flaw in the system. The lists took so much time to maintain that I had no additional hours for chores.

"Did you forget the laundry this week?" Husband asked one morning. "I'm out of socks."

"They're drying in the oven," I told him. "The dryer's broken, you know."

"Didn't you call the repairman?"

"According to my schedule, I make phone calls on Tuesdays. This is Thursday."

"It's ridiculous!" he fumed. "Wasn't that course supposed to help you get organized?"

"I *am* organized," I protested. "I know exactly what I'm supposed to be doing. I just can't find the time to do it."

I shared my plight at class that evening, and everyone nodded sympathetically (there were only four students left). We all seemed to be having the same trouble.

Fortunately the teacher understood. "You've got the basic premise," she assured us. "Now it's just a question of putting everything into practice. Might I suggest signing up for Time Management? Just down the hall, room twenty-three."

Instead I enrolled in Vegetarian Cooking. I might as well

produce something interesting at the stove, in addition to all those dry socks.

> The ordinary arts we practice every day at home are of more importance to the soul than their simplicity might suggest.

—THOMAS MORE (1779–1852)

12 Remember the Rose

I realized during my childhood—when the doctor diagnosed my "asthma" as an allergy to cats and dogs—that I was not cut out to be a pet owner. My sense of frustration deepened during the first years of my marriage, when even the hardiest houseplant withered at my touch. Our children had the distinction of being the only preschoolers in the neighborhood whose turtles always died on the way home from the pet store. Obviously the poor things had come in contact with me.

Being the natural Kiss of Death to any living organism had never really bothered me. I honestly had no deep-seated affinity for animals, being the type that would rather retrace my steps than pass that frisky unleashed German shepherd up ahead. And although I sighed over the cheery greenery featured in decorating magazines, there were always silk plants available, which even I couldn't overwater. But basically, the need to nourish something (other than a clutch of perpetually starving offspring) is inherent to the nature of most women. And so, last year, I tried again.

It all started during the summer when, quite unexpectedly, one of my rosebushes bloomed. My children heralded the unexpected news throughout the neighborhood and before long, neighbors began storming our backyard, eager to behold the miracle with their own eyes. In the midst of the champagne toasts, my mother arrived, took a long look at the blossom and offered her bewildered congratulations: "How did this happen?" The next day she presented me with an ivy cutting and, as proof of her continuing trust, advised me that she would be standing by, available for midnight phone consultations.

So! I had a real houseplant! And except for one crucial day when Mother felt compelled to take it home for an overnight stay in her plant Intensive Care Unit, it seemed oddly contented with me.

As we settled into winter, I decided to put up some shelves in the den. We did need space for our books, but the ivy was now sporting a real vine, and I could picture how impressively it would dangle over the volumes. While I was taking measurements, a daring thought evolved. "Don't you think a little fish tank would look sweet on one of those shelves?" I asked Husband.

He eyed me suspiciously. "With fish in it?"

"Of course. I could put a tiny lamp on top. Indirect lighting, you know."

"*You* want to raise fish?"

"Remember the rose," I advised him.

The idea of a small fish tank did not appeal to my husband, but the idea of a large one did. For Christmas, he and the children presented me with a twenty-gallon aquarium, filter system, pump, artificial plants, fluorescent lamp, colored gravel, minicastle and their prayers. When one of us eventually thought to put water in it, the tank became too heavy to rest upon the new shelves. I removed one of the shelves and bought a stand for the tank. It looked beautiful, gurgling contentedly in the corner. "Why don't we leave it like that?" the five-year-old asked, no doubt remembering years of deceased turtles.

"Oh ye of little faith," I chided, herding them into the car for our trip to the pet store. "Remember the rose!"

We purchased seven tropical fish as a start. "You'll need food," the pet store manager told us. "And a how-to book," his assistant mentioned helpfully. "Be sure to buy a net and an algae scraper," advised an elderly lady who had stopped in to have her dog's toenails clipped.

Our fish seemed happy enough in their new environment. And the shelves above the tank seemed a cozy place to store all their supplies. I moved the ivy to a higher shelf where it could converse with our new philodendron—a congratulations gift from my son's teacher, who had heard about the rose. Gradually, however, some of our finny friends developed a curious rash. I called a neighborhood teen whose tanks were flourishing.

"Ten drops once a day," he prescribed, handing me a medicine bottle. "Mrs. A, I know you grew that rose all by yourself, but you really need some help with these fish. For one thing, you should have a tank heater."

"And a thermometer," his buddy pointed out.

The pet store manager agreed. "Take some antibiotics home too," he told me. "Try changing the filter," his assistant advised.

"Say," asked a customer who had stopped in to buy a duck, "aren't you the lady who grew that rose?"

Depressed at having to spend that week's meat budget on fish supplies, I cheered myself by pausing at the plant counter to buy a geranium. Hopefully, the sight of it would cheer my ivy, which had been looking a little brown lately.

Thoroughly medicated, in water heated to a healthy temperature, two of the fish died immediately. The rest hung bravely on, gazing at me with great mournful eyes. The philodendron began to droop.

About a week later, I came into the den to find my husband thoughtfully surveying the aquarium. "You know," he said, "this whole corner's beginning to depress me."

I followed his gaze. The fish were dancing crazily at the top of the tank, bumping into dead geranium leaves that bobbed on the surface. "All our books are still stacked in my closet," he went on quietly, "and we've spent more on this hobby than we did on the last baby."

I left him the job of dismantling the corner, murmured sincere apologies to St. Francis, and wandered out to the garage. I'm not exactly good at admitting defeat. And besides, I wanted to see if there was any rose fertilizer left. After all, it's almost spring.

Nothing would be done at all if [we] waited until [we] could do it so well that no one could find fault with it.

—JOHN HENRY NEWMAN (1801–1890)

13 Put a Little Culture in the Family

I felt a little guilty when the psychologist at the grade school open house suggested that we parents spend more time enriching our children's home environment. I had been so busy keeping the gang from playing in traffic, making sure they ate green vegetables and teaching them their nighttime prayers that I had slipped up on this critical facet of parenting. I was determined to rectify my error and thought the best place to introduce a little culture was probably the dinner table—an assembly that needed all the help it could get.

"Tonight," I announced as the first glass of milk went over, "we're going to discuss something intelligent for a change. Since two of you are currently studying fables and maxims in school"—I had sneaked a peek at their homework to come up with a likely topic—"I'm going to toss out some sayings, and you try to guess what they mean."

Several pairs of eyes darted away from the nightly battle-for-the-ketchup-bottle and fastened upon me. "Sort of like a riddle," I explained further, ignoring their puzzled expressions. "How about 'All that glitters is not gold'?"

Chewing noisily, the group pondered. Second Son had a thought. "That means that people who have a lot of things usually don't have any money."

Eerily accurate. Had he been inspecting our charge account balances? I pressed on. "Who knows what is meant by 'Kill two birds with one stone'?"

"Who would kill a bird?" Daughter demanded indignantly.

"Oh, sweetheart, that doesn't really mean—"

"But you said—"

"Don't ask her if it rained cats and dogs last night," Husband murmured, trying to keep a straight face, "or if she's taken the bull by the horns lately."

I sighed. This experiment was obviously not going according to plan.

Our eldest child decided to be helpful, as he often does—regarding himself as a third parent. "Our teacher asked yesterday what 'Nothing ventured, nothing gained' meant."

"What did you say?" I encouraged him.

"I told her that was what Dad said when he climbed the weeping willow tree to cut down those branches."

"I remember that!" Youngest beamed. "We all wrote our names on his cast!"

"Never mind," I interjected. Husband was looking grim. "And get your arm out of the salad. Let's try something a little different. I'll start a saying, and you tell me how to finish it."

Second Son tossed tomato bits at the cat; Third looked ready to fall asleep; and the rest of the clan—well, this enrichment business was a lot harder than I'd anticipated. I could only wish the school psychologist would pop in to offer his wisdom. (Did he even have offspring of his own?) "Try this one," I pressed on. "A rolling stone——"

"Can break your basement window!" Second finished, remembering, no doubt, a particular episode last summer.

"Not quite," I answered brightly. "Try again. 'A penny saved——' "

"No one saves pennies, Mom," Eldest informed me loftily.

"You can't buy anything with a penny," Daughter agreed. "And if you put it in your bank, it just lies there and gets rusty."

"Speaking of money, Mom,"—Eldest looked up from his fourth helping of pasta—"you owe me four dollars and sixty-five cents, remember? From pulling those weeds last year?"

"You owe me a quarter, Mommy," Second Son added, "from when I helped you vacuum and dust and wash all the spider webs off the corners because you were crying because Aunt Emmy was coming because——" He stopped as his elbow toppled another glass of milk. *Why don't we just feed it to them intravenously?* I wondered.

"Give it up," Husband told me under his breath. "There may be a method to your madness, but trying to instill any culture into this bunch is a wild-goose chase."

"You're right," I hissed back. "They're all chips off the old block. Why should I cast my pearls before swine or try to make hay while the sun shines? Talk about being down in the dumps!"

As I cleared the dinner wreckage later, I had to admit defeat. My clan is lovable but, let's face it, not very enriched. And why should I be surprised? As I'm sure the school psy-chologist would agree, "By my fruits, you shall know me."

To the outside world we all grow old. But not to brothers
and sisters. We know each other as we always were. We know
each other's hearts. We share private family jokes. We remember
family feuds and secrets, family griefs and joys.
We live outside the touch of time.

—CLARA ORTEGA

14 The Play

She's a daffodil in the school play, Lord. All month long she has practiced her two lines, murmuring them endlessly as she drew pictures and nestled with her teddy bear. All month she has allowed me to fit the yellow-petal creation to her little body, only rarely lapsing into typical kindergarten impatience. "Is it almost the day, Mommy?" she asked me only this morning. "Is the play almost here?"

It is, Lord, it is. But it's her mother who has the stage fright.

I sit here in the school auditorium, surrounded by the noisy chattering crowd, waving to friends, and the butterflies bounce and thud within me. She is so small, Lord, so very vulnerable in this, her first exposure to the scrutiny of her world.

Before today I have kept her close to me, safe and sheltered, guarded from possible rejection or failure, secure as only a deeply treasured child can be. But time passes, Father, and now she must spread her fledgling wings, enter an alien world, one I can share only from a distance. Don't let her fall, Father, not this first important time. She is so very small.

A rustle from the back—then the kindergarten children come down the center aisle, flushed and shyly proud as our beaming attention focuses on them. And there's my daffodil daughter, pink-cheeked and searching as she nears my chair. Can she hear my worried heart beating?

Then for a moment our eyes meet, and I see my own pride reflected in her face. "Hi, Mommy," she whispers as she passes. "I love you."

The children are on the stage now, but the dark red curtains blur before my eyes. For once again, a little child has led me. Why did I not see until now, Lord, that love is a bond that transcends all boundaries? Why did I not understand that my daffodil will never be alone, that she can face rejection, pain—yes—and joy too, for she is deeply rooted in my love, and in Yours.

The play is about to begin, Father. Thank You so very much.

> Children require guidance and sympathy
> far more than instruction.
>
> —ANNE SULLIVAN (1866–1936)

15 A Star Is Born

Over the years lots of people have asked how I got into the lecture business. Okay, so *you* haven't asked. But I'll tell you anyway because you may decide to join me on the circuit someday. It's a great part-time job, and there's always room for new faces.

I had been freelancing magazine articles from my tiny desk upstairs. And for some reason (we didn't have enough to do?) a friend and I decided to combine our talents and coauthor a family humor book. Shortly after its publication, we were invited to a local radio station to promote it. Wisely my coauthor declined, but I—looking for a way to get out of the house—accepted. Almost immediately, I regretted my haste.

"What'll I *say*?" I whimpered to the host a few minutes before airtime. "What if someone phones in with a question I can't answer?" My knees were developing a peculiar twitch, and a large herd of butterflies had taken up residence in my chest.

"You'll be fine," the host soothed. "Just be your usual, hysterically funny self."

But I'm not hysterically funny, I wanted to explain. That's just a hat I don when I'm writing family material. Actually, I've got all the humor of the Middle East, especially before 7:00 AM. And if I'm so entertaining, how come the kids call me Sarge?

But it was too late. The On Air sign flashed, and we were off and running. Somehow I managed to hide my terror behind a barrage of witticisms about the kids' making Jell-O in my washing machine, finding socks stiff with rigor mortis and harvesting a bean crop from the soil in my carpets. The call-in audience didn't challenge me with any brainteasers either; they simply wanted to swap stories about *their* bean crops or ask how to get bubblegum out of a dog's ear. All in all, a delightful experience, but when it was over, I was definitely relieved. Now I could go back to being Gertie Grumble. I was wrong.

That afternoon, some lady phoned. "I heard you on the radio," she said, "and I'd like to know if you would speak to our women's club next month."

"Your women's club?" I echoed. "Oh ... well, I'm sorry but I don't speak."

There was a pause. "Then what were you doing on the show today?" she countered.

"Well ..." It was a good question. "Actually, I was just ... talking."

"Exactly. That's what we want you to do for us. And be hysterically funny, of course."

"But . . ." What would I talk about? I wanted to ask. Would I be able to get up in front of a group of real people and say anything at all? Being on the radio is different; you can always pretend that no one is listening, and quite often, that's true.

Then again, imagine! A room full of people who actually *wanted* to hear what I had to say, who would not respond to me with "Uh, later, Mom," or "Can you cut it short, dear? I have an appointment for a root canal."

Then the caller mentioned the magic phrase: "What's your fee?" and as they say, a star was born.

Over the next few weeks, I learned the difference between "talking" and "speaking." Talking was something I did all day —random comments not apt to send passersby into spasms of glee. Speaking, on the other hand, demanded a carefully planned and practiced outline with a point to it, accompanied by merry asides, all carefully honed, delivered clearly—while maintaining good eye contact—and with perfect timing. And worst of all, memorized.

"I need a title too," I moaned one night to Husband. "What am I going to call it?"

"How about 'How Did I Get into This Mess'?" he suggested.

"Clever. Why don't you give the speech, Mr. Witty?"

On the day of the talk, I arrived early, hid behind a potted plant and prayed fervently that the group would suddenly remember a bus tour that they all wanted to take and cancel out. I didn't trust myself more than six feet from the ladies' room, and the butterflies were back, doing a mating dance across my chest. Sadly, I thought of all the jobs for which I was eminently well suited: school bus driver, prison matron, cafeteria helper, maid. Why, in the name of heaven, had I become a writer?

But it was too late. The chairwoman was introducing me, and to a burst of warm applause, I clutched the podium, stared into the sea of expectant faces (so many faces!) and began. And suddenly . . . it was all right! They listened thoughtfully, laughed in the right places and even charitably clapped at the end. And they opened a wonderful door for me, an opportunity to break up my solitary writing career with an occasional excursion that brought me a renewed enthusiasm (and more material) as well.

I spoke locally for a while and then acquired an agent who mentioned that she'd like to book dates for me in other parts of the country. "Not a chance," I told her in a panic. "For one thing, I don't fly. For another, most of the kids are in school now, but they still expect meals every day. I have to put traveling on hold until I go on Social Security."

Then my agent mentioned the magic phrase: "Your fee would increase.'" And, as they say, one must go with the flow.

Hesitantly I broke the news to my beloveds. "Mother's going on a little business trip," I announced casually as the after-school horde tumbled in. "A convention has asked me to provide a spouse program for them and do some media."

"Great, Mom." They yawned. "What's for dinner?"

I phoned my husband. "I'll be flying to Virginia next month." He put me on hold.

Getting organized for my two-city tour required preparations reminiscent of the Normandy Invasion. I wrote seventeen stickum notes and stuck 'em. I laundered everything that wasn't permanently attached to something else. ("Gee," mused Husband, "I haven't seen this shirt since our honeymoon.") I froze enough meals to feed an entire Cub Scout den, complete with warming instructions attached. I counted the ice cubes.

"You really don't have to do this, you know." Husband watched as I disinfected the driveway. "It's no big deal. Any normal man can take care of a family for a few days. It's just a matter of organization." (Somehow, things had never seemed that uncomplicated to me.) "You just have a good time." He patted my shoulder. "We'll hardly notice you're gone." And with those heartening words ringing in my ears, I left.

At least twelve hours passed before I broke down and turned on my cell phone, in a television station green room. It rang immediately. "Hi," Husband said. "I just finished cleaning the inside of those louver doors in the laundry room. They were loaded with dust. Don't you ever vacuum back there?"

"And hi to you," I responded. "How are the kids?"

"The kids?" He sounded blank. "Oh, they're around somewhere, I guess. Today was a school holiday so I put them to work washing the walls."

"Today was not a school holiday." My blood pressure was starting to rise. "And why do the walls need washing?"

"Well, it was the darndest thing. You know that blender,

the one with the missing blade? I was mixing some ketchup and cracker crumbs, you know, for the meat loaf, and all of a sudden—"

"Wait a minute. I left you a meat loaf with ketchup and cracker crumbs already in it." My voice was rising and the television show producer was frantically motioning to me.

"Yeah, but when the oven overheated, the firemen ended up throwing it out—"

"The firemen?"

"Hi, Mom, how's the trip going?" My high school sophomore was on the upstairs extension. I heard Husband stealthily hanging up.

"What on earth is going *on*?" I demanded. The show's theme song was playing and I should have been in the studio, but I was flipping through my itinerary. If I skipped tonight's speech and caught a red-eye, I could be home ten hours sooner.

"It's been interesting, Mom. Did you know that if you put applesauce and bleach down the same drain at the same time—"

"Hon, never mind. What's happening with Dad?"

"He just left. I think he's crying. And the principal called to tell you that Brian can't count his superman costume as a school uniform."

Eventually I returned home, a little bit wiser and much older. I would continue to take my trips, I decided, stuffing my guilt at leave-taking and reminding everyone that this was all for our benefit. Not only would my own disposition (and the family budget) benefit, a short break from one another now and then would make all our lives a little richer too. "We've missed you," Husband whispered.

"Don't go away again, Mommy," said Third Grader. "I hate meat loaf."

Those magic phrases. Aren't they hysterical?

Absence makes the heart grow fonder.

—AUTHOR UNKNOWN

16 Wanted: Just One More Closet

When you have a family, you have an abundance of clothes. And if one considers the woman-hours spent in comparison shopping, purchasing, laundering, storing, mending (does anyone do that anymore?), ironing (does anyone do that anymore?) and keeping track of clothes, it's a wonder any of us have time for our novels and bonbons.

Clothes start out as a fun experience. What expectant mother doesn't delight in her first baby shower, oohing and aahing over doll-sized yellow sleepers and teensy undershirts? Don't the items look sweet, all neatly stacked in drawers of Mother's choice, or carefully dropped into a laundry hamper when damp and juice-stained? Such images should be enjoyed to the fullest, because they definitely won't last.

By the time a child is two or three and must accompany you to the store to be fitted, shopping tasks take on a new perspective.

"Sneakers! I want sneakers!"

"No, honey, we're here to buy good shoes for church."

"Green and yellow sneakers!"

"Stop screaming. They're $39.95 and they don't go with anything you own."

"Sneakers!"

"And you have a perfectly good pair at home."

"Pretty, pretty sneakers!"

"Well, maybe I could find a green outfit to match. They are cute, aren't they?"

Two hours and seventy dollars later, you arrive home, only to discover that Toddler has had a change of heart. "Don't wanna wear sneakers! Want church shoes!"

Most middle-sized kids abhor shopping and submit only because there's a chance they might snag a hot-fudge sundae (or some time at the video games) as a maternal reward for their suffering. By the time they've reached teen status, however, kids can happily make a career out of browsing and trying-on. This would be nice if Mom could stay home and catch up on her e-mails, but it doesn't work that way. If an unsupervised teen daughter is instructed to purchase a plain white shirt, four pairs of kneesocks and a warm sweater, she will return with a plaid vintage skirt—indistinguishable from the other plaid vintage skirts in her closet—and a tennis outfit. ("But, *Mother-r-r*, the new tennis coach looks like Matt Damon!") Hence, shopping mall benches are littered with middle-aged moms staring glassily into space, waiting for daughters to decide between four identical white shirts. "Mom! Wake up, Mom! They don't have a thing I like. Let's check the Jean Jungle."

Once brought home, clothes must be properly cared for. I'm all in favor of teaching kids to do their own laundry, but a parent must watch this situation closely, at least at the start. One thing you will notice is that a novice washes only the item he is currently concerned with and will usually fill the water level to Extra Large.

"What do you mean, you washed your red baseball socks with Dad's white shirts?"

"Well, they were in the machine already, and you told me not to just wash one or two things—"

"Never mind. If your little brother was in the machine, would you wash him?"

"Probably."

Kids' clothes also have the annoying side effects of tearing (never along the seams), losing buttons, and developing knee- and elbow-holes and damaged zippers. If one lacks a degree in professional tailoring, and Grandma no longer remembers how to thread a needle, the answer is a wicker basket—set cozily by the TV—into which all damaged merchandise may be tossed. Theoretically, on slow nights Mother can "relax" by sewing on a button or three. Since there are few slow nights in the average American family, this system has an added advantage: Left in the basket for a few months, the clothes have all been outgrown and can be passed along, with a perfectly clear conscience, to one's sister-in-law.

Storage of clothing presents another challenge. It's all very well to suggest that each family member have his/her own closet. But experienced parents know that stuff expands to fill the space available. And further, no matter how huge a closet, there is no guarantee that Child's apparel will end up there. "Hi-kids-how-was-school-hang-up-your-coats" is a standard late-afternoon greeting in most homes, followed the next morning by "Mom, have you seen my hat-pants-left-gym-shoe-and-coat?"

Storage gets especially tricky when several folks share a too-small house.

"Mom, will you come up here and look at *his* side of the room?" Ten-Year-Old bellowed last week.

Obligingly I stared at his roommate-brother's heap of clothing, scattered all over the floor. "I just did everything in your hamper yesterday," I told Brother. "What's all this?"

"My laundry."

"But it was clean yesterday."

"It's still clean."

"Then why don't you shove it in your drawers?" Ten protested. "I need space for my electric train setup and my gerbil cages."

"There's no room in my drawers." Mr. Mess opened each one—each jammed full of garments I hadn't seen in years.

"Why, that's your First Communion suit," I murmured, "and your T-ball uniform—"

"I quit T-ball three years ago," he pointed out. "Mom, can we fix this?"

If only we could. If only I could figure out a way to keep track of all the apparel that passes through our lives. Did I buy this pink jacket for Little Sister or is she on another trading binge with her best friend? Who belongs to this huge pair of athletic shoes, and why are they on the top of the refrigerator?

Clothes do make life interesting. But sometimes I find myself dreaming of a desert island. Just the family, a barbeque pit and a change of bathing suits.

A mother rearing children … is forced, almost against her will,
to constantly stretch her heart. For years… her time is never her own,
her own needs have to be kept in second place and every time she turns
around a hand is reaching out and demanding something. She hears the
monastic bell many times during the day and she has to drop things
in midsentence and respond, not because she wants to, but because
it's time for that activity and time isn't her time, but God's.

—Father Ron Rolheiser
The Catholic Northwest Progress

17 Housewife Trapped in Frozen Foods

I was standing in the supermarket checkout line. I'd been there so long that a passing stock boy was marking my lettuce down to half price. To pass the time, I perused those sleazy tabloid headlines: "Woman Gives Birth to Twelve Babies, All Redheads." "Loch Ness Monster Spotted in Backyard Wading Pool in Dayton." "What You Don't Know about Pizza Can Kill You."

I was just sneaking the issue of my choice under the lettuce when I realized that my neighbor, Glenda Glorious, was in line right behind me, eyeing the blaring banner with a lifted eyebrow. "I'm buying it for the miracle cranberry diet," I told her. "See? The one that says you can lose twenty pounds by Easter."

"You've only got another twenty-four hours," said size-five Glenda, glancing at my mismatched sweat suit with ill-concealed distaste. "I don't think you're going to make it."

"These marshmallows are on sale if you buy a second bag," the checker yelled in my direction. "Want to go for it?"

"Why not?" I sighed. There's always next Easter.

That's the trouble with supermarkets. You can't keep a secret there. All anyone has to do is glance in your cart, and your life becomes an open book—or in my case, an open box of pretzels. Worried about your weight? The whole world knows as they peruse your whitefish and celery content. Feeling blue? It's chocolate toffee bars and a cake loaded with trans-fatty acid. Budget a little strained? Maybe no one will notice that we seem a bit top-heavy on lentils and peanut butter this week.

Supermarkets have other problems too. Did you ever notice how often they shuffle the products around? I can tell you, whenever I've got the layout memorized and can race down aisle eight to grab a forgotten can of tuna, careen around the corner to aisle six for bread and sprint to the end display for mayo—all in a moment flat—that's when the stock boys get bored and decide to play their version of Frustrate the Customer. Tomato paste? "Oh, that's now over in section four, ma'am, right next to the detergent."

Of course. How silly of me. Tide next to Tomato.

Then there are the decisions to make. Grocery shopping was once simply a means for people to restock empty kitchen larders and keep families reasonably nourished for another week. But now the job requires credentials. First, we must spend hours reading labels. Salt content? Too high for Husband who, although he is still consuming the usual amount of gumdrops each week, has decided to cut back on salt. Calories? Too high for Teen Daughter who will shriek, "*Mother-r-r-r*, you know this is going to make me fat!" about anything you bring in, including bottled water. Sugar content?

Too high for Son whose orthodontia is overtaking the national debt. Of course, a day after I have totaled a receipt taller than I am, all of my loved ones will cheer my efforts with the same comment: "There's nothing here to eat."

I've tried clipping coupons. Once I actually did save six dollars on a ten percent discount sale running between 7:45 AM and 8:00 AM. But my savings were on houseplant fertilizer (we rarely own any living plants), strained infant liver (we don't own any babies) and books to help save me even more money. (Although *Weaving Cloth for Fun and Profit* and *Root Canal for Dummies* left a lot to be desired.)

I don't do well with mathematical calculations either. If peas are priced at two cans for $2.19 and frozen bean boxes weigh ninety kilograms each, shouldn't I just buy broccoli? If I have a fifty-cents-off coupon on Cereal X, a newspaper ad for a two-for-one margarine sale and a buy-one-buy-the-second-at-half-price store special, shouldn't we all become vegetarians?

I have another responsibility too. Not many people know about it, but it's my job to throw the checkout scanner out of whack so it reads all my prices wrong, forcing me to challenge the totals and endure the sighs, eye-rolling and "Oh, I don't believe this!" remarks of the thirty people in line behind me. Occasionally, without even knowing about it, I can break the scanner completely, forcing the checker to call the manager so both of them can stand around, poking it with metal gadgets and saying, "Gee, it was working this morning" or "No, we've already started to ring you up; you can't move to another register."

Just yesterday I tossed a couple of cans of beets onto the conveyer belt and braced myself as the electronic device beeped harshly and refused to compute. "They're forty-nine cents each," I told the clerk. "I'll just give you a dollar and five cents for the total and tax."

"Sorry, I can't sell anything until I know the price," she told me, sliding the cans back and forth across the stubbornly mute beeper.

"But I know the price," I told her. "Just let me give you a dollar and—"

"I've got a ninety!" she shouted in that ominous consumer code, and the loudspeaker echoed my crime. Shoppers turned to glare at me.

"Funny." The manager glided over. "It was okay this morning."

I looked at the woman in line behind me. "Did you bring something to pass the time? Counted cross-stitch? Your will? The guest list for your son's wedding?"

"My son is three years old," she said crossly. Her ice cream —buy three, get one almost free—was beginning to thaw.

"It'll probably take that long," I told her. "Or wait a minute. Have you seen that new cranberry diet? The one where you can lose twenty pounds by Easter? It's worth a read."

"Thanks," she grabbed the Loch Ness monster issue. "I've been meaning to check it out."

If only we could.

Joan's Kitchen Rules

- Dinner is ready when the smoke detector goes off.

- If you eat something and no one else sees you eat it, it has no calories.

- Half that many noodles makes oodles.

18 What Is a Twelve-Year-Old?

I was a guest on a local Happy Homemaker TV audience-participation show and the moderator unexpectedly asked me what age was worst for a boy.

"From the kids' point of view or ours?" I asked.

"From a mother's perspective, I guess," he answered.

I didn't need to ponder. "Twelve," I announced promptly. The audience (all moms) cheered.

"Okay, then when is a *daughter* at her worst?"

The audience joined me this time. "TWELVE!" Democrat, Republican, blonde or brunette, size four or twenty-four—we were in total harmony. These preteen years are the most challenging of all growth stages.

What makes a twelve-year-old so perplexing?

He's a child of contradictions, suddenly taking four showers a day (last year we had to introduce him to a bottle of body wash) and flying into a panic if his hair hasn't been shampooed since morning. But his bedroom is a veritable sty, with last week's stale jeans mixed in with the balled-up sheets and blankets. His feminine counterpart doesn't make sense either. Her closet is packed so tightly with garments that it's becoming a fire hazard but, according to her, she has nothing to wear.

Remember those cozy mother-daughter chats, cookie-baking sessions, shopping trips, flute duets? They've gone. Miss Twelve is now in a period of chronic humiliation, the cause of which is apparently her mother. You who were adored and imitated by a younger daughter are now a constant source of embarrassment to this same female. Cries of "Oh, *Mother-r-r-r*, you just don't understand!" ring through a previously peaceful household, accompanied by the now-familiar racing-up-the-stairs-and-slamming-the-door routine. Mom's clothes are old-fashioned, her hairstyle dated, her attitude feudal and her mere existence a problem. It does little good to reassure Mom that by the time her daughter is sixteen, Mom will have to keep her makeup and clothes under lock and key and buy earplugs for relief from Daughter's incessant chatter. What counts, unfortunately, is today—and how to stay sane with a Twelve in residence.

A preteen son, while less vocally dramatic or critical, is just as aggravating. He now scorns his father's invitation— "How 'bout going for a milkshake, Buddy?" (after all, what if the gang were to see him in public with his *father*?)—and he wouldn't be caught dead carrying on a conversation with anyone older than eighteen. While he'll burn up the telephone lines with his peers, he develops a startling reticence around the house. "Huh?" "Who, me?" and "Pass the potatoes" is about as chummy as he gets. It falls to Mom to explain to younger siblings that Twelve's "you dummy!" is actually a term of endearment.

Twelve is a materialistic age—never again will the correct

label on a pair of sneakers be so significant. Our preteens keep the national economy humming with their absolute need for video games, a complete wardrobe update every few months and fashionable sports equipment. When parents suggest that their offspring earn the cash for these goodies (or at least spring for the difference between labeled items and K-Mart specials), Twelve is apt to go into cardiac arrest (or shift into the classic run-upstairs-and-slam-the-door scene. According to Twelve, Mom and Dad owe him not only love, food, shelter, clothing, schooling, movie tickets, orthodontia, immunizations, contact lenses and music lessons, but also an annual vacation (the Cayman Islands in January will do), a home chemistry lab and the latest in designer jeans. Standing firm against many of these "musts" develops Mom's mental muscles and makes Dad suddenly very busy at the office.

What inexperienced parents are just beginning to learn about Twelve has been recognized for years by the educational system. That's why preteens are usually quarantined from the rest of civilization and herded into middle school buildings where—it is fervently hoped—their obnoxious behavior will not infect the "normal" kids. Here, in a domain all their own, they pursue the same puzzling behavior, spending their days shrieking and giggling, explaining why they didn't have time to do their homework, eating pizza for breakfast and lunch, starting an argument with their best friends, complaining about science class, pasting pictures of Hollywood role models on their lockers and commiserating about the discipline at home. Middle school teachers are easily recognizable at PTA functions—they wear earplugs (to block sound), have a peculiarly hysterical laugh and always maintain loudly that they *love* teaching sixth and seventh graders. (Thank You, God.)

It's no surprise that a Twelve is barely tolerated in his neighborhood. It is he who is still throwing a basketball into a hoop in his driveway at 10:00 PM. It is she who will play lovingly with the younger kids on Tuesday, then refer to them disparagingly as babies on Thursday. Fortunately, many households have either lived through a Twelve or are going to be doing it someday, so parents sigh in exasperation, look the other way or commiserate with each other about the discipline at home.

Twelve can be a brutal experience, and perhaps the one hardest hit is the child. Being Twelve is an emotional rollercoaster ride, with newly emerging hormones whirling in unpredictable patterns. No longer a child, yet not ready for adulthood, feet suddenly too large and emotions shaky, hair a different color every day and an unreliable voice, testing authority yet needing security as never before—Twelves are vulnerable, uncertain, angry, scared and perplexed. If your Twelve was once a nice person to know, this attribute will most certainly return; eventually the skies will clear and a calmer, surer, more delightful young adult will emerge from the turbulence, someone who will be our pal forever.

What can we do with our Terrible Twelves in the meantime? Stand firm, pray a lot—and love them.

Before I got married I had six theories about bringing up children; now I have six children and no theories.

—JOHN WILMOT (1647–1680)
SECOND EARL OF ROCHESTER

19 My Sister, My Friend

ristotle said friendship is composed of a single soul inhabited by two bodies. Cicero believed it was the only thing in the world that all humankind could agree was useful. And Jesus told us that the greatest love of all is to lay down one's life for a friend.

While all friendships are special, everyone knows that gender gives them particular flavor. Men seem to have side-by-side friendships, built around doing something together, such as bowling, painting a house or complaining that their wives and children don't understand them. Women's friendships, by contrast, are more face-to-face, cemented primarily by conversation, sharing and venting that their husbands and children don't understand them. "What do you talk about all night?" my husband is apt to ask as I tiptoe into the bedroom after an especially fulfilling night out with the "girls." I can only shake my head and smile into the darkness, remembering how we give and take and grow rich in the exchange.

I suppose that's why it's hard to pinpoint the true meaning of friendship, at least for a mom. But because I believe it should be celebrated, I'll give it a try.

A friend is someone you can phone at eight thirty on a Monday morning to say you're dropping off your two toddlers in about ten minutes—and she will say okay, and not ask why.

A friend is someone you hope will be at the next meeting of the book club or PTA committee, because somehow it's always more fun when she's there.

A friend is someone who meets your eye and goes into gales of laughter at the same time you do—and usually at the most inappropriate moments—and no one else can understand exactly what is so funny.

A friend is someone who will ask your advice—and sometimes even take it.

A friend has a way of making you feel like Rachael Ray at your own dinner party—even though the only thing you ever serve is roast beef.

"Peggy," I whisper into the telephone one traumatic morning, "I'm having a terrible problem with the three-year-old. He's developed this habit of teething on the baby."

"You poor kid," Peggy says, while pulling her preschooler out of the oven. "Have you tried chloroform? Now when mine was that age . . ."

A friend is someone you sometimes miss—without knowing exactly why.

A friend will lend you her only evening wrap and not even ask you to be careful with it.

A friend won't think you're terrible if you once threw your wedding ring at your husband. If your husband threw it back, she won't think he's terrible either.

A friend is someone who brings her own glass of iced tea to your kitchen because she can't stand your coffee.

"Camping isn't the right vacation for you," my sister tells me on the phone. "Your idea of roughing it is watching black-and-white TV."

"Or having to bring my electric blanket," I add.

"And who wants to play Count the Cows on a four-hundred-mile trek?" she points out. "This year, you're all flying to my house. Have pool and air-conditioning—will share."

A friend is someone who listens to what you say and hears the message hidden underneath the words.

A friend is someone who knows her children aren't perfect and doesn't care if you know it too.

A friend is someone you can tell to go home.

A friend is someone who will tell you about the spiders in her kitchen so you can tell her about the mouse in yours.

A friend will unexpectedly take your children to the pool because she thinks you need a nap.

A friend is comfortable, reassuring and sometimes messy. She laughs easily, shares her tears and occasionally uses bad judgment. A friend understands and accepts you the way you are but is loyal enough to tell you when you're behaving like a child.

Your friend may be your mother, your daughter, your sister, a pal from kindergarten or someone you met at last year's church picnic. Whoever she is, she's more precious than you will ever know. For God so loved the world that He sent us friends, to reflect His infinite love in their eyes.

How truly blessed we are.

> Friends are the family we choose for ourselves.
> —EDNA BUCHANAN

20 Marvelous May

May should be the "merry, merry month." To me, it's more like "scary, scary." As every parent knows, that's because May is the most expensive month of the year. (And you thought it was September or December, you dreamer.) May is serious money. You can plan for some of it, but it's those unknown variables that are apt to throw your budget into a spin.

For example, about ninety-five percent of the engaged couples we know schedule their weddings for May. At least it seems that way. Never mind that there are eleven other months—well, in the Midwest, about three other months—that are eminently suitable for orange blossoms and "Here Comes the Bride." It matters not. May, somehow, is the only time to start a marriage on the proper footing.

One doesn't panic. One simply collects the invitations, hangs them on the hallway door, and the seasonal argument begins with Spouse over which weddings to attend.

"It'll have to be Fred's daughter on the fourth," he announces firmly. "Fred and I used to be best friends, you know."

"In the fifth grade," I point out. "We've never laid eyes on Fred's daughter. They must be hard up for gifts. Can't we just send her a set of silver swizzle sticks and go to your nephew's bash instead?"

"Were you planning to wear your going-to-a-wedding dress to our nephew's ceremony?"

"Of course. I always wear it. But—"

"And again the following week to our niece's marriage?"

I see his point. The same people would be at both functions. They'd probably show up, too, for the two christenings, First Communion and golden anniversary party scheduled for the end of May. This would mean I'd need new outfits so I wouldn't be in all the photos wearing the exact same thing, which would be great, but with the charge cards overextended because of silver swizzle sticks and other presents . . .

Some people with budget problems and schedules regift, that is take something they were given and couldn't use and threw on the top shelf in the garage, rewrap it, and present it to the guest of honor as if the item were brand-new. It may be a practical solution, but given my memory problems, what if I inadvertently return a gift to its original donor? Would she ever speak to me again? Would I speak to her?

"I've got it!" I say. "Let's both break our legs in April!"

We can't, of course. There's no room in the checkbook for orthopedic services. Not in May, when school winds down and the little educational "extras" begin to appear.

"I need eighteen dollars for a science book I lost last February."

"I need $4.50 to replace a busted combination lock. And seventeen dollars for overdue fines at the school library."

"I need sixteen dollars for the softball bus fee."

"I need five dollars for a present for Sister Mary Gruel. She's retiring, you know."

"I thought she retired last year," I point out.

"She retired from teaching last year. This year she retired from running the school cafeteria."

I can't blame her. A quiet convent always looks good about this time of year, even to me. Especially if our eldest is graduating.

"I need twenty dollars for a Senior Dress-up Day necktie and the car" (presumably for gas) "for the class picnic" (likely to be held in a neighboring state). "I need a new suit to wear under my cap and gown—by the way, the gown rental's sixty-five dollars—plus thirty-five dollars for pictures, thirty-eight dollars for the yearbook, twenty-five dollars for Mary Rose's corsage for the prom—"

"Let me ask you something." I throw Mr. Six-Footer against the wall. "Why did you wait until the very last minute to inform me that you are graduating?"

"Mom, I've been in high school for four years, on the honor roll. I thought you'd figure it out." He pats me on the head. Why is he so tall?

"Well, I can't be expected to remember everything," I huff. "And where's all the money from your job at Merlin's Meat Market?"

"In the bank. For college. And by the way, I need fifty-five dollars for a duffel bag and a new alarm clock and a couple thousand for my first installment on the dorm housing fee."

If one can stagger through the last days of school, there are still banquets to be faced and financed. I welcome any chance to eat someone else's cooking, but the eighteen-dollars-a-plate "special" loses its thrill when the whole family wants to attend.

"You kids can fix your own hotdogs tonight. Dad and I are going to the band banquet."

"You mean we're not going? We're not going to see our little sister get the Most Improved Musician award?"

"Or hear her play 'Flight of the Bumblebee' on her tuba?"

"You've heard her play it a million times," Husband points out. "In fact, you've been begging her to stop."

"Oh, Daddy, let them come," pleads Little Sister. "After all, I'm going to their sports banquet. And your bowling dinner. Aren't I, Daddy? Huh? Aren't I?"

And need we mention the added expense of spring gardening, the bags of lawn fertilizer, the flats of marigolds and pansies, the refurbishing of the lawn mower, painting the old porch furniture, new tires for the car and registration fees for summer activities (at least their library cards are free).

There ought to be a law. Folks should band together and declare May permanently banished from the calendar.

But then we'd miss the sweet, tentative breezes hinting of slow and lazy moments yet to come, the joy of Mother's Day, the promise in the eyes of a bride and groom. We'd miss the fun, the laughter and camaraderie of family, the pride when one of our own achieves something wonderful. Yes, and we'd miss the bills too. For May, more than any other month, makes us believers in God's providence and care, secure in the fact that whatever comes, He will see us through.

I wouldn't miss a marvelous moment of it.

Creating a family in this turbulent world is an act of faith,
a wager that against all odds there will be a future,
that love can last, that the heart can triumph against all adversities
and even against the grinding wheel of time.

—DEAN KOONTZ
FROM THE CORNER OF HIS EYE

21 Regrets

THINGS I WISH I HAD NEVER SAID

"It's just a little pain, sweetheart. Stop complaining!"

"I wonder how I'd look as a redhead."

"Of course I can have the article finished by Saturday."

"If he gives you any trouble, Mr. Principal, you just let me know."

"Certainly Daddy can drive your team to the game tonight."

"Honey, you seem a bit edgy lately. You aren't mad at *me*, are you?"

"Well, if you're sure they're both girl hamsters, I guess you can keep them."

"No, the check won't bounce. I made an online deposit yesterday."

"I'm going to the store—anyone want anything?"

"It's up to you."

THINGS I WISH MY HUSBAND HAD NEVER SAID

"Just hand me that hammer, hon. I'll have this fixed in a jiffy."

"Put on the steaks at six o'clock, and I promise I'll be home at 6:05 PM."

"I met Al and Mary at the hardware store and invited them over tonight. We aren't doing anything, are we?"

"Running a house is simply a matter of proper organization."

"Let's see . . . fit Part A into Sprocket B . . ."

"I know it's the wrong color, but it was marked down fifty percent."

"Boy, you women have it made."

THINGS I WISH THE KIDS HAD NEVER SAID

"Hey, Mom, what's this funny rash on my leg?"

"I've decided to try out for football this year."

"Guess what? The whole second grade can come to my birthday party."

"Let's make Mom breakfast today."

"These new shoes are already too tight for me."

"Wow! Look at all that blood!"

"Want to see me jump off the high dive?"

"I promise I'll feed him and walk him and brush him three times a day! You won't even know he's in the house!"

"Some lady called you, Mom. She sounded real excited."

"If God is everywhere, how come you said He lives in church?"

"Mom, if I tell you this, promise you won't get mad?"

Yes, Lord, I know we all talk too much. But at least You're always there to listen.

We all have enough strength to bear the misfortunes of others.

—FRANÇOIS DE LA ROCHEFOUCAULD

(1613–1680)

22 How to Survive Summer

hat are you doing?" Husband asked nervously, eyeing the hammer in my hand.

"Relax." I smiled. "I haven't thought up any home improvement projects for you. I'm just posting some rules in the kitchen."

"Rules?" He stared over my shoulder at the hand-lettered chart.

"For summer vacation," I explained. "So we'll have a little sanity around here."

"Impossible. Then again, these are rather interesting."

"Aren't they?" We both studied the poster:

SUMMER RULES

1. Teens sleeping later than noon shall be considered comatose and will be resuscitated by the paramedics (in full view of the entire neighborhood). Children under five years of age are requested to stay in bed until dawn.

2. Since the chauffeur resigned last week, all offspring are required to take walking lessons and will assemble on the front lawn for practice. It's simple once you get the hang of it. Bicycle riding is strongly encouraged, provided it is not done in the dining room. Management suggests you get in shape for said walking/cycling activities by running errands, cutting grass and taking out the garbage.

3. On those rare occasions when licensed drivers are given permission to use the car, please understand that "come in early, dear," does not mean "early in the morning," nor does permission to buy a sweatshirt imply that the purchase may be made in Omaha.

4. Mud pies may not be stored in the refrigerator.

5. Since the cook quit last week, the following routine shall be established in the kitchen:

   + Crumbs shall be wiped up. (Clutch dampened sponge, move arm in circular motion.)
   + Dirty dishes shall be carried to sink and rinsed. (Turn small silver object to On, hold dish under water flow.)
   + Items removed from refrigerator shall be returned to same. (Clutch item, put one foot in front of the other. Repeat. Open door. Place item on shelf.)
   + No more than two guests shall be invited for lunch each day, with sworn affidavit that your lunch will be provided the next day at *their* house.
   + Food labeled DO NOT EAT shall be left intact.
   + Fishing worms (even in covered containers) may not be stored in the refrigerator.

+ Anyone caught drinking an entire gallon of fruit juice during a twenty-four-hour period shall pay his own hospital bill.

6. In regard to lost beach balls, tennis rackets, stuffed animals, swimsuits and sandwiches, the management suggests you bypass her and go directly to St. Anthony.

7. All library cards shall be renewed, all downstairs hamster races discontinued. Telephones will be answered by the management only between the hours of midnight and 6:00 AM. No lemonade stands shall be set up before breakfast.

8. Since the maid retired last week, certain rules regarding the second floor will be observed:

+ Under no circumstances may bedrooms be shared with anything remotely resembling a reptile.

+ Stale socks and jeans crammed under the bed and not retrieved for thirty days shall be fumigated and then sold for storage fees.

+ Wastebaskets shall be emptied while it is still possible to lift them and before stale apple-core aroma permeates curtains.

+ If room air conditioner does its job too well, do *not* switch on furnace to neutralize. Instead, search for small button on air conditioner labeled OFF. Press.

+ Showers shall be limited to one per day per person, fifteen minutes maximum. Telephone calls not permitted while showering. Hair dryers have been confiscated until the onset of cold weather and will then be ransomed. Small children are asked to collect all plastic boats, bubble pipes and other paraphernalia from bottom of tub. (Daddy is still recovering from sprained ankle.)

9. Due notice shall be given the management concerning Brownie campouts, Little League playoffs, picnics, dentist appointments and other events where her presence is required. "Due notice" is interpreted to mean "more than ten minutes."

"Not bad," Husband remarked. "This chart certainly covers most of the basics."

"Most?" I asked. "Did I leave anything out?"

"Just hand me that crayon," he said, and wrote:

10. The garage shall be off limits to all minors. No one is allowed to borrow contents of tool box, test the snowblower, hang ice skates from the rafters, draw hopscotch patterns near the lathe or play in the fertilizer.

11. The morning newspaper will not be confiscated for paper dolls or perusal of the sports section until *after* breakfast.

12. Finally, broken bones, stitched chins, concussions, dental cavities and diaper rash are strictly prohibited until fall, in order that Head of the Household can catch up on bills resulting from an especially active spring.

"Very good," I enthused. "You've certainly caught the spirit."

"Yes, but do you think it will do any good?" Spouse asked.

"Maybe not for the kids," I admitted. "But I'm feeling better already."

"Me too." He grinned. "Hand me that hammer."

I rant, therefore I am.

—DENNIS MILLER

23 You Are Cordially Invited

The first party I ever threw as a newly-wed was so dull that even my husband left. On another occasion, the merry-making awakened our toddler who proceeded to throw up on the guests' coats, which had been tossed casually across our bed. During our third anniversary bash, my husband decided at the last minute to barbeque the meat outdoors, and I served dinner at 12:45 AM. With a record like that, only a fool would keep trying.

But I do. Somewhere there must be a magic formula that makes entertaining as simple as changing a diaper, and a lot more fun. However, I haven't found it yet.

Other women don't seem to have this problem. One neighbor can feed her husband's bowling team on a moment's notice simply by thawing the marvelous homemade goodies always stacked in her freezer. Another sets her table with gleaming crystal, untarnished silver and real roses bobbing in a bowl of pink water. My most recent centerpiece—a plastic daisy in a pickle jar—didn't seem to have the same appeal.

Part of my dilemma stems from a confused sense of priorities. Should a hostess focus mainly on her house—making sure that guests do not spy water pistols in the bathtub or dirty socks sticking out from under the china cabinet, thus encouraging their imaginations to run rampant as they wonder what they are *not* seeing? Or is a beautifully served dinner the most important component of a gracious evening? Once I managed to accomplish both of these feats simultaneously, but since I had forgotten to invite anyone, the evening lost much of its luster.

One must also tread gently when making up a guest list. I once asked three couples from our new neighborhood over for wine and cheese and discovered as the doorbell rang that two of them hadn't spoken to each other in years. It was a very brief soiree. On another occasion, my mother brought her elderly maiden aunt over on the same day we had asked a family with eight children to picnic with us. Fortunately, my great-aunt has a sense of humor and a hearing aid that she kept turned to Off throughout the day, or it could have been a disaster.

Theme parties present a unique challenge: selecting and arranging appropriate decorations. It helps if a hostess is naturally creative and has good finger coordination, but I have only recently learned to press the On button on our washing machine and would not classify myself as especially inventive. Buying a batch of Happy Birthday napkins is about as festive as I can get, especially if they get misplaced and end up being used for Valentine's Day.

Since we have the largest family within my clan, we usually host the holiday get-togethers, and these, too, have had their disastrous moments. One of the problems is that stray relatives—and even complete strangers—seem to pop up at the last minute, necessitating a quick shuffle with place settings and extra instant broth in the soup. Such miscalculations can result in favorite uncle Bob being seated in the laundry room for Thanksgiving dinner because no one remembered he was coming. Then too, my female relatives are all gifted—and interested—in the kitchen. I'm the only one who finds it impossible to recite the recipe for curried rutabaga from memory, or whip up a scratch wedding cake while watching *Oprah*. They smile kindly over my barbequed-beef-and-gelatin menus, but I suspect their hearts are not really in it.

Friends, on the other hand, have all accepted this deficiency in my character and are always willing to help in a crisis or suggest potluck, if they will be invited. One incredibly patient pal lends me her handmade papier-mâché stork whenever I give a baby shower and insists on assembling my punch. She sincerely believes that although mixing ginger ale and sherbet may seem easy, with me, one never knows. Another talented neighbor antiqued my old dining room tabletop, convinced that glamorous surroundings would inspire me to new culinary heights. She was wrong.

In spite of my bumbling efforts, people seem to enjoy coming to our house. Perhaps it's because they are genuinely welcome and able to relax and be themselves. Perhaps it's also because the women will eventually discover my messy coat closet, gritty soap dish or frozen pies and realize that, as hostesses, they have no competition from me. Whatever the reasons, we consider ourselves fortunate to have so many interesting (and tolerant) guests. I may never discover that magic formula, but it's always a thrill to hear someone say, "We had such a good time at your house. When are you guys having another party?"

Maybe I ought to check the calendar.

It is easy to get so caught up in living life that we forget how simple it is to touch another person, how necessary and meaningful it is to experience the sharing of loving acts.

—BONNIE BLOSE
HOST OF *BOOKS AND BEYOND*

24 Just a Moment of Your Time...

I have been involved in politics since I grew up in Chicago where my father was one of the handfuls of Republican precinct captains in a ninety-eight percent Democratic city. In vain we stuffed envelopes and accompanied Dad to meetings attended by three or four souls who came mainly for the doughnuts. "Why are we doing this?" I once asked him. "Our candidates never win."

"That's why," he explained. "This will teach you how to be a gracious loser."

He was right. And it also taught me why voting opinion polls have value. Usually I'm willing to cooperate. But is it my imagination, or is the Information Highway far more crowded than it used to be?

Yesterday I drew the line. "As you know, our local elections are scheduled for next month," the voice on the telephone informed me, "and we'd welcome your opinion. If the election were being held today, would you vote for ...?"

"I'm really not familiar with most of the candidates for Mosquito Abatement Director," I interrupted her apologetically.

"It's summer, you know, and the kids get to the newspaper before I do. They're building a papier-mâché fort in the backyard and—"

"But you *have* to have an opinion," she insisted. "How am I going to fill out all these forms if you don't choose a candidate?"

"You pick one," I suggested generously. (She had an honest voice.)

I don't know if she did, but her dilemma points up an interesting facet in today's society: Everyone is supposed to have an opinion—on everything. And further, we're supposed to share our ideas with those who want to know. In many cases, these nosy people are even willing to pay us for expressing our views.

I was running through a shopping mall recently, a neighbor's four-year-old in tow, when I was practically tackled by one of those clipboard-and-horn-rimmed-glasses types. "Can you and your little boy spare a moment to take part in a short taste test?" She smiled through brilliant teeth. "It'll only take a few minutes."

"I have to pick up the kids for lunch," I blurted, thinking fast. Taste tests at this mall have been known to last all afternoon, and involve delicacies like spinach or beets.

"It's only ten o'clock." She dismissed me and leaned over to grip an uncertain Michael. "You'd like to take a taste test, wouldn't you, honey?"

Michael looked at me for his cue. I shook my head firmly.

"It's chocolate pudding," the interviewer cooed, turning her charm to Full Speed Ahead.

"Chocolate pudding! Oh boy!" Michael was delighted.

"And the test pays ten dollars," she added for my benefit.

"Ten dollars?" I brightened. "Well, I guess we can spare a few minutes."

"Wonderful." She whipped out her ballpoint. "Now, can you give me your son's full name?"

"Oh, he's not mine. I'm just watching him this morning for his mother. She had an abscessed tooth, and—"

"Sorry." The entire mall must have heard her notebook snap shut. "Only mothers and sons for this interview. You don't qualify."

"But I want pudding!" Michael started to sob. Several shoppers shot dirty looks in my direction.

"Pudding!" By now it was a wail. A security guard moved forward as Ms. Perfect clicked away on her nine-inch heels. Needless to say, I spent the rest of my precious shopping hour consoling Michael at the food court.

Which brings me to another observation. The companies that commission these consumer tests apparently don't ask *everybody's* opinion on their latest product. No, before being asked to spout off, one must qualify by running through a series of preliminary queries.

"Have you had your hair cut anytime during the last decade?" a recent researcher asked me. "Do you use grated cheese on your salads? Is your home heated with wood?"

"Yes, yes, and our home isn't heated with anything right now," I answered. "It's eighty-five degrees out, and even though the nine-year-old did turn the furnace on yesterday, it was just because he was bored. There's nothing to do in the summer, you see, and—"

"Never mind," she interrupted. "Can you be here tomorrow for a thirty-minute survey on paper napkins? It pays twelve dollars."

"Why not?" I said. "It'll cover the gas and get me away from the nine-year-old." It's not only the kids who get bored.

It's rather interesting (and flattering) to live near an opinion research office and to be asked so often to share our views. My teens have offered commentary on video games and sports equipment, Spouse has voiced his preference on shampoo and beer—a memorable evening that led to a two-week silent period in our home—and if I qualify, I sometimes drop by to view a test commercial and then fill out a questionnaire: "The commercial you just viewed was (a) exciting, (b) persuasive, (c) clever and witty, (d) all of the above?" Unfortunately, there's not always space to say what one really thinks.

Then, of course, there are all the telephone polls. "Are you listening to the radio right now?" a sweet voice inquired.

"Not really listening," I began to explain. "Someone turned it on this morning and then went off to baseball practice. I haven't gotten around to turning it off. It's buried under a pile of dirty beach towels."

"And to what station are you listening?" she pressed on.

"WBAD."

"And why do you prefer that station?"

"I don't," I told her. "The dial is stuck there. You see, the nine-year-old—"

"Never mind." The click echoed through the house.

I suppose I should feel gratified that there are so many people Out There hanging on my every pronouncement, who pursue me through the highways and byways of life just to record my pizza preference or political persuasion. But I admit to being stumped on one point.

If my ideas are so important, how come no one at home is listening?

> One advantage of talking to yourself is that you know at least somebody's listening.
> —FRANKLIN P. JONES

25 The Field Trip

The bus is late from the field trip, Lord. I've been waiting here at the park entrance, watching for the comforting sight of the large yellow vehicle chugging into view with its precious cargo of eight-year-olds. And it hasn't come.

We were supposed to be here at 3:00 PM, Father, to pick up our campers. I can still see their elated faces as they climbed up the bus steps this morning, whacking each other with lunch sacks, overjoyed that the long-awaited zoo trip had finally begun. We adults were smiling too, Father, remembering day camp adventures from years long past, savoring the children's excitement as if it were our own.

But it's 3:45 PM now, Lord, and the bus isn't here.

It's strange how all mothers' hearts beat to the same rhythm. Anxious eyes scanning the horizon, we move together in a small protective cluster, as if this unconscious act could ward off the dangers threatening to invade our world. Each woman's thoughts travel the same path. *Are they lost? Has there been an accident? Lord, keep them safe!*

Strange, too, how these moments of doubt increase our own vulnerability, our awareness that we are helpless to control even the smallest detail. And yet the thought brings a sudden rush of peace. For You are intimately in control, Father, watching the flight of the sparrow, numbering each blade of summer grass, holding our children's hands as well as our own.

I glance at an unknown mother standing across from me, and our eyes meet. *It will be all right*, I tell her silently from the depths of my renewed courage. *It will be all right. He is watching.*

Suddenly someone points, and the rest of us laugh and move away from each other, embarrassed at the intensity of our relief. The bus is coming, Lord. You have brought our little ones safely home.

Thank You, Father, for this small lesson in faith and for Your never-ending protection and love. Thank You for our eight-year-olds who will enliven tonight's dinner tables with rapturous accounts of giraffes and baby alligators, giving glory and triumph to this ordinary day. Thank You for mothers who can speak the language of the heart, sustaining each other when no words come.

And most of all, Father, thank You for a big yellow bus.

One can endure sorrow alone, but it takes two to be glad.

—ELBERT HUBBARD (1856–1915)

26 Those Who Can, Teach

One of the careers I am definitely unsuited for is the hallowed profession of teacher. It's true that for years I've been instructing novice writers at our local junior college adult education unit (with the grand title of Adjunct Professor), and my class is always filled to the brim. But there is a major difference between my adult students and the smaller kind one meets in most schools: My students want to be in the classroom. And because they're motivated—even turning up with paper, pens and eager expressions—teaching them how to get published is a joy.

Not so with the younger set. I am awed and slightly baffled by those parents who homeschool, or actually choose to share classrooms with little people; frankly just the scent of all that peanut butter, on a daily basis, would make my teeth tingle. But there's no accounting for taste—or talent. Teaching is a gift, one that I apparently missed. Although I can *tell* children what to do, I find it almost impossible to *show* them.

For example, it's impossible for me to demonstrate the art of tying shoestrings. Today's parents may not understand this dilemma because small-fry shoes most often utilize Velcro, which takes the place of silly laces with even sillier bow-and-knot arrangements. But in the era when all first grad-ers needed a working knowledge of laces as well as language arts, my kids were always on the brink of being held back for more practice. Gamely I would schedule lessons: "See, honey, you hold this part in this hand and with your other finger—No, not that one, this one . . . I think . . . yes, you bring this piece around . . ." To complicate matters, one of the boys is left-handed and I had to reverse the process for looping (as well as remember to put him at the left corner of every table we gathered around). But it didn't matter. None of the kids ever had the slightest idea of what to do. Inevitably some favorite visiting uncle would take pity on my floppy-shoed tot and show him (in one brief lesson) how to master the skill. That also went for telling time on a clock with arms instead of a digital readout.

Perhaps my helplessness stems from childhood when I never progressed further than Beginner Ping-Pong at the local park and was always the last one chosen for playground games. Without any background or experience, why should I now know how to be a sports authority simply because we created a few people who wanted to be players?

Of course, I didn't realize on that fateful day when our firstborn joined Little League that this was to be my lot in life. It seemed like a harmless pastime—good healthy exercise—and besides, it was the one sport I could follow somewhat intelligently. My enthusiasm waned quickly when Son was named pitcher of the team and expected me not only to catch for him during backyard practice but also to signal his pitches.

"Mom, didn't you call for a strike? How come you dropped it?"

"I was scratching my nose. And why is this ball so tiny? What happened to those big squishy things?"

"That's softball, Ma. How 'bout another strike?"

"WAIT! The baby's running across home plate!"

My husband, with a great deal of tsking and head-shaking eventually took over Son's coaching. And that was fine with me. Not only am I still unable to throw an item farther than a foot or two, the thought of looking up into a bright sky, picking out something falling toward me, and actually performing the physical mechanics required to be under that object as it lands in my outstretched palm is a feat difficult to comprehend, much less master.

Relieved of coaching baseball, I was just in time to learn the finer points of basketball with Second Son, at that time the shortest boy in fifth grade. It didn't take us long to realize that Second had inherited my tendency to stumble while moving, and even though he developed a rather interesting skip (which brought him down the court in record time), he never learned how to stop to make the basket (nor could he toss it that high). This did not endear him to the coach. All coaches seem to feel that theirs is the only extracurricular activity that matters, leaving kids to do homework—the *purpose* of school—at midnight, but that's another story. When Second received his squad dismissal slip, I was a bit disappointed. I had just figured out what a personal foul was (I had thought they were accusing Second of bringing a chicken to practice), and it seemed a shame to waste the information.

"Foul!" I shouted out the back window at my two oldest sons. "You get a free throw, Tim."

"Mom, we're boxing," Older explained patiently. "In this sport, you're allowed to touch each other."

"Well, it looks dangerous to me. Just play for one quarter."

The boxing didn't last long and (mercifully) neither did ice hockey. After only four trips to the emergency room for stitches, split lips and first aid on a chipped tooth, the boys packed away the skates, pucks and sticks, along with balls, bats and mitts. Second returned to his first love—science projects—and built us a replica of the human heart, which I used as a centerpiece on the dining room table.

The others discovered the sport of gentlemen: golf—a harmless pastime, plenty of good, healthy exercise (where have I heard this before?) and no parental involvement expected. Except getting up to drive them to the links at 5:00 AM so they could manage a quick eighteen holes (or is it rounds?) before school. Except relinquishing the hall coat closet to golf bag and shoe storage, and stepping around makeshift putting greens set up on the kitchen carpet. Except prying those little tees out of the washing machine fan belt and cautioning a budding Tiger Woods about to take a full swing in the living room: "WAIT! The baby's right behind you! And look out for the lamp!" The bright side: Becoming caddies enabled the group to finance their equipment and fees.

Instead of following in his brothers' footsteps, Youngest Son introduced me to a new game.

"What's that thing?" I asked him one morning.

"A tennis racket, Mom. I bought it at a garage sale."

"What's it for?"

"To play tennis with. Haven't you heard of Dinara Safina?"

"Sounds like a disease. And stop slamming that ball against the stove!"

"That's how you play tennis, Mom."

"That's not how you play it *here*."

So Son retired to his room for the next few years. When he wasn't on the court (or is it "diamond"?) he treated us to the steady beat-beat-beat of ball against wood paneling, which he cleverly adjusted to beat in tandem to the heart. Husband took to wearing earplugs, and I counted the days until Son would be eligible to join the National Guard, while I starched his regulation white tennis shorts and tried to figure out what a score called forty-love could possibly mean.

Daughter, of course, remained my ray of hope. For years she disdained anything rougher than tree-climbing, and though she learned to leap off the pool high dive board before she was six, she showed no interest in team sports or anything remotely resembling equipment. And then, my bubble burst.

"What's that piece of paper, honey?"

"It's a permit slip, Mommy. For soccer."

"But—"

"I'll need shoes with cleats. And shin guards."

"But—"

"And can you kick the ball to me so I can practice defense? I'm goalie."

So this is how I'm spending this summer. Screaming at referees. Toting ice for bruised knees. Trying to decide if this is the first set or the second hole of play. Or maybe the third inning or the fourth quarter?

I'm signing up for ladies' bowling. If you can't beat 'em, I always say, you might as well strike them out.

> While we try to teach our children all about life,
> our children teach us what life is all about.
>
> —AUTHOR UNKNOWN

27 Over the River and Through the Woods

Taking a family vacation is much like getting married: It seems like such a good idea during the planning stages. By the time the launch is only hours away, however, I find myself praying that a swarm of locusts, the bubonic plague or some other act of God (why is God only credited with disasters?) will cancel it all.

Part of my prevacation jitters stems from the fact that Spouse and I can never agree on where to go. This man, who hasn't glanced at our bank balance for the past five years, blithely decides that since we vacation so rarely, we ought to do it right when we have the chance. Whistling cheerfully, he consults the travel section of the newspaper, talks to folks in the office and phones every chamber of commerce within five hundred miles. "Listen to this deal on houseboating down the Mississippi!" he's apt to enthuse, or "How about flying everyone to the Grand Canyon? Al took his family out there last summer and they had a great time!"

I resist the impulse to point out that Al's family consists of his wife and their fourteen-year-old daughter, who probably spent the entire trip listening to her iPod and grunting when they addressed her. Our gang proves more of a challenge. Do we really want our three-year-old playing on the side of a cliff? Do we really want to spend our entire IRA on airfare? And how do we feed ourselves once we've landed?

"I was thinking of a weekend visit with my sister in Dubuque," I point out timidly. "We could save on motel bills by sleeping in her wine cellar."

"Dubuque? All that corn?" Spouse snorts. "Where's your sense of adventure?" *Probably buried somewhere in the over-due bills drawer,* I think to myself. After a few spirited discussions, however, we compromise on a modest getaway. The next challenge is to pack.

I'm not very good at this kind of thing. I've learned that one cannot pack clothes too far ahead because children keep needing to wear the same items right up until we pull out of the driveway. But one should not wait to pack until the last minute either. There have been trips when Husband had to purchase pants because I forgot all but the pair he was wear-ing. He does his own packing now.

One must bring games, carsick crackers and of course DVD players, tapes and Game Boys to keep the kids occupied as the miles add up. We also need cotton balls to stuff in adult ears when the backseat refrains consist of "When do we eat?" "I gotta go—*now!*" and "*Mother-r-r-r,* he's looking at me!"

Even if I were good at it, packing a food chest for a seven-hour drive is a test of anyone's ingenuity. Items can't be kept in our refrigerator long enough to be wrapped for the trip unless we hire an armed guard. To overcome this problem, I usually hide goodies around the house as I buy them and assemble the collection five minutes before takeoff. This is a good system, provided one remembers that the Limburger cheese is hidden in the piano bench, or that Spouse specifically asked me to bring along some pickled herring. But the effort is worth it when one considers the alternative: allowing preteen sons to step inside a roadside diner. ("Sure, I can eat five hotdogs, Dad." "So can I." "So can I. . . .")

Although we usually drive, there have been those occasions when Gram and Grandpa accompanied us. And since nine people in a five-seat sedan seems like overdoing the family togetherness, we sometimes split up. One year all male members of our expedition took the car, while Gram, little Daughter and I decided to travel via jet. It seemed a fabulous idea 'til we discovered belatedly at the airport that all flights were cancelled until further notice. Our men had a wonderful time, they tell us. But sitting in a terminal with a four-year-old who sang "The Teddy Bear's Picnic" approximately seven hundred times (interspersed with "Is this our vacation, Mommy?") is not a thrill I'd like to repeat.

Packing the car presents hurdles as well. Should we stash luggage, tricycle, golf clubs and rabbit hutch in the trunk? Or stash the aforementioned in the backseat and position children in trunk?

Timing our takeoff is crucial; we can't hit the road during the same week that the junior high sidestroke finals are scheduled. Nor should the kids have to miss the annual garbage can derby (an extravaganza of dented metal and broken teeth), the block party or the carnival. Nor can we miss the senior citizen soccer playoffs (Grandma's goalie this year). We must be sure that no one has been exposed to chicken pox or worse, and be certain that we've disconnected the utilities for the duration. (I'm always tempted to make this a permanent arrangement.) After we've taken all of this into consideration for the one-and-only week we can all get away, Husband discovers that he forgot to reserve his vacation time at the office, and the whole procedure starts again, along with sullen silences and "If some people would just pay attention . . . "

Despite chaos and the occasional is-this-really-worth-it? blues, we're sold on the family vacation. Whether sharing a modest lakeshore cabin with compatible pals or staying for a blissful weekend in a luxury hotel, the break in routine is good for us all. The kids experience new sights, the pleasure of ordering from a menu and a revived closeness with the most important people in their world. Mom and Dad add to a storehouse of fond family memories and learn what kind of trips they'd like to repeat alone next time. Vacations are the jelly on the bread of family life, the cement that binds our yesterdays. Whatever the difficulties, they are well worth it.

So I guess I'll dig out the backpacks and the Sunday travel section once more. As Spouse mused only yesterday, "Wonder if they're chartering flights to the moon yet?"

No matter what happens, travel gives you a story to tell.

—JEWISH PROVERB

28 My Personal Wish List

I met my friend Perfect Peggy at the mall a few weeks ago. Peggy isn't really perfect—I'm sure she has a hangnail now and then like the rest of us—but she seems to accomplish so much with such effortless grace. She'd be an easy person to hate, but in addition to all her other attributes, she's nice too.

"What have you been doing lately?" I asked her, which was a mistake.

"I painted the house last week," she told me proudly.

"The inside?"

"The *outside*. Scraping that trim near the chimney was murder!" She laughed merrily while several mall-walkers turned to admire her chic tennis outfit and slim legs, nicely tanned. "Let's see. My barbershop quartet won the regionals, so we're on our way to the national competition in Hawaii. And my summer school class in Ethiopian literature is lots of fun. How about you?"

"Me?" I mentally reviewed my world of unmade beds, Scout campouts and pregnant gerbils. "Oh, the same old stuff, I guess."

She studied me through heavy (natural) lashes. "You need a wish list, Joan."

"A wish list? What's that?"

"You write down everything you've always wanted to do, pick one item and get going on it *now*."

"Is that how you manage to accomplish so much?" I asked her.

Peggy shrugged modestly. "I decided a long time ago not to wait for that perfect someday. Why not try to brighten my life now?"

I nodded thoughtfully. Her philosophy certainly made sense, especially if one looked forward to painting houses. My life was definitely on hold, and not likely to improve—unless I was willing to do some personal work on me.

That night I started a wish list. After writing madly for a while, I read with a critical eye. "I want to be a single career girl" was my first entry—a little late here, considering the existence of the kids. Nor had I worked in an office since before pantyhose were invented. Besides, it really wasn't an honest wish. I long for single status only on desperate days. My family is truly the best part of my life. Scratch number one.

"I want to take a bubble bath alone." On the surface, this seems a reasonable request. But I have yet to convince the kids to knock before entering, or better still, to take long naps while I'm lolling under the foam. At one time, I decided that a lock on the door would solve my problem. But after summoning the fire department twice in two days to rescue the toddler who had locked himself in, I abandoned that strategy. Besides, is this the kind of thing Peggy would put on *her* list? Eliminate wish number two.

"I want to learn how to swim." I have never told this to anyone, but I am the only adult female in the history of our park district's existence to flunk Beginner Wading. It was an accident, really. I hadn't signed up for the class; I was simply there to pick up my five-year-old from Advanced Diving. But when I saw him dancing on the end of the high board, I became hysterical. I ran forward to catch him, fell over the edge of the pool into a class of splashing babies and was tossed out of the park by an angry lifeguard. "No sneakers, no sunglasses and no ice cream bars in the pool!" she snapped. "Next time read the rules!"

"I wasn't—"

"And besides, you haven't *registered* for wading."

After writing down this wish, I phoned the park, but the lifeguard still remembers me, and she's been promoted to chief instructor. She said I couldn't come any closer to the pool than the concession stand until I learned to wade. Imagine being treated that way by your own daughter.

Forget item number three.

My next goal seemed more doable. "I want an office of my own, complete with potted plants, a working printer, my own phone line, file cabinets and a door with a deadbolt lock."

"I never knew that was one of your burning ambitions," Husband remarked, looking over my shoulder.

"That's because I never complain about anything," I replied virtuously. "But part of caring for others is caring for yourself too. And do you think it's easy handling the household paperwork—to say nothing of my writing business—from a drawer in the pantry?"

"But we can't spare a whole bedroom. Where would the kids sleep?"

"Next door?" I asked hopefully.

He frowned. "How about tossing all the boys in one room? What's an extra bed in all that debris?"

My eyes shone. "You mean . . . ?"

"Sure." He put an arm around me. "Everyone needs some space."

Peggy was delighted when she heard the news. "This is just the beginning," she assured me. "Today an office, tomorrow tap dancing lessons, next year mountain climbing."

"I'll settle for my very own stapler," I told her. "Thanks, Peggy. You really are perfect."

She blushed. "Not really. I'll let you in on a little secret. I've gained three pounds this summer."

I hid my shock. After all, people don't have to be perfect in order to be lovable. And I can learn a lot from Peggy. Next time, *she's* going to make my wish list for me.

I love people. I love my family, my children . . .
but inside myself is a place where I live all alone
and that's where you renew your springs that never dry up.

—PEARL S. BUCK (1892–1973)

29 A Lemon by Any Other Name

With our eldest earning an A in Driver's Education class (plus one middle-aged matron who was getting awfully tired of going back and forth to the grocery store on roller skates) it was inevitable that our family would add a second car. In fact, the only member who was not ecstatic about our decision was the Head of the House. "Gasoline costs money," he pronounced sagely, with the assurance of one who will drive to the corner mailbox rather than risk wearing out the soles of his twenty-year-old work boots.

"But we'll only be using the car in times of dire need," I pointed out, keeping a straight and earnest face. "Like getting the boys to work, hitting the underwear sale at Sears, racing a pneumonia victim to the hospital, my Tuesday night prayer group ..."

"I see." Husband nodded seriously. "Just bona fide emergencies. No cruising up and down streets looking for high school parties, or serving dinner in the backseat because of the little kids' soccer game schedules."

"Exactly."

"As soon as we can afford it," Husband said.

"Since when has that ever mattered?" I snapped. "We're living in suburbia now, remember? The neighbors pick up milk for me and chauffeur the kids around. I'm beginning to feel like a leech."

Whether fate intervened or St. Christopher took a personal interest in my traveling problems I will never know. But sometime later, an ancient green sedan, christened Betsy, became a member of our family. Battle-scarred and rusty, she wore her dents proudly and delivered us to our destinations in a trustworthy manner, at least at first. But when the flu season hit and she developed a cough more raucous than any of our offspring's, I decided rather belatedly that perhaps she needed a checkup too.

Betsy was admitted to the nearest auto emergency room for tests. It was almost two days before the mechanic summoned up enough courage to call me in for a consultation. He was obviously in a state of extreme agitation, and I tried my best to put him at ease. "Just give it to me straight, Al," I told him staunchly. "What's wrong with Betsy?"

"Well . . ." He swallowed convulsively. "Have you noticed that when you apply the brakes, Betsy immediately swerves into the oncoming lane?"

"Of course," I reassured him. "That's why I humor her by staying under fifteen miles per hour."

"And do you think," he went on, a bit glassy-eyed, "that her steering seems a bit loose?"

"The wheel revolves four or five times for each turn," I pointed out proudly. "Not many cars can match that record!"

"And one of the back tires isn't touching the ground anymore." Al sighed gloomily.

I leaned forward earnestly. "Can Betsy be saved, Al?"

"I'll do my level best," he promised, "but you'd better look into a second mortgage, or at least a full-time job."

I shrugged, checking the estimate. "Where can you get a car in good running condition these days for a paltry $968.70?"

Betsy was worth every penny of our overextended budget, and shortly after being released from Intensive Care, she redeemed my faith by once again transporting us around town, her little engine humming happily. At least that's what my husband and sons told me. I was only allowed to use the car between the hours of 2:00 AM and 6:00 AM on Wednesdays and Fridays, which made it difficult for me to hear Betsy's $968 purr.

"Look," I tried to explain to Spouse one morning. "Betsy is supposed to be my car, and I'm planning to claim her on my income tax as a dependent. Why, therefore, are *you* driving her on all these little errands?"

"It's easier than taking the plastic wrap off my car," he explained. "And besides, you have Betsy most of the day."

"Oh really?" I answered sarcastically. "For your information, I haven't seen Betsy since last Thursday. If the boys aren't taking their friends to the movies, then it's baseball practice or—"

"The boys?" he interrupted, stunned. "Do *they* still live here?"

"Who do you think just passed us on a five-minute pit stop?"

"You mean that large person who grabbed the leftover ham bone and your gasoline credit card was . . ."

I nodded solemnly. "Our oldest."

By threatening to put the teens up for adoption, I eventually reclaimed daytime custody of Betsy, and during the next several months she made many new friends for our family. As I'd chug past Sam's E-Z Drive, he would often wave and yell, "Need a tow today, Mrs. A?" When I filled up at the corner station, the attendants—by now, on a first-name basis— would pat Betsy's fender affectionately and inquire after her carburetor. And when a neighborhood teen mechanic discovered that I had had a new muffler and brakes put on, his concern was really touching. "You didn't," he kept murmuring and shaking his head. "Tell me you didn't throw good money—"

I shrugged. "Where can you get a car in decent running order for a paltry $719?"

Eventually, however, our final crisis came. Betsy's power dwindled to that of a golf cart, then the transmission failed and she would chug only forward but not in reverse. "We could put in a circular driveway," I suggested to Husband. "That way, I wouldn't have to back out whenever I ran away from home."

"Out of the question," he snapped.

"But where can you get a car in good running order for a paltry $3,000?" I asked.

"Plenty of places," he told me. "And I suggest you start looking—now."

We left Betsy at a nearby auto graveyard where they strip

cars for parts. Our six-year-old played "Taps" on her kazoo, but the gesture didn't banish my tears. Even the dealer's promise to bury Betsy under a headstone shaped like a lemon left me unmoved. Silently, I turned away and headed for the exit, stopping only as we approached a small red convertible sagging inconspicuously in a corner of the car lot. I stared at her as the kids surrounded me.

"She has a certain dignity, doesn't she?" I murmured.

"I'll say!" gushed the eighth grader. "No windows to get dirty and that chartreuse door's really cool."

"And look, Mommy," added the six-year-old, "her headlights keep winking on and off. Isn't that cute?"

After all, as I told Spouse later, where can you buy a car in good running order these days for only $19.95?

Never drive faster than your guardian angel can fly.

—AUTHOR UNKNOWN

30 It Is September

I can hear the dust settling. I can hear the plants growing. Look, look, Mommy. Look, look, Spot. The children are gone.

It is September.

I used to feel guilty when my favorite month rolled around. After all, doing cartwheels down the supermarket school supply aisle or humming "Happy Days Are Here Again" while cramming sandwiches into brand-new Dora the Explorer lunch boxes is hardly the way a proper mother should greet the fall. If I really *cared* about my children, goes the admonition of the child psychology experts, I would be consumed with grief at the thought of the lonely hours awaiting me. I would be plunged deeply into the throes of an Empty Nest Syndrome or, at the very least, a mild midlife crisis. And if I couldn't summon up any of these reactions, surely tact demanded that I refrain from tap-dancing around the kitchen on the first day of classes—at least until the kids had left the kitchen.

Well, as my favorite aunt used to say, "Piffle!" I do care about my children—enough to realize that if I spend one more humid day in their presence, I may become manic-depressive. Or they might. Families can stand just so much togetherness before it becomes necessary to call in the Peace Corps. And the start of school, coming when it does, is the perfect reprieve. Kids can drive *other* adults crazy for a change. And parents can reacquaint themselves with the more civilized aspects of life—eating on dinnerware that does not collapse as soon as food has been placed there or showering without a layer of sand in the bathtub.

And so, that is why, during the waning days of August, I faced the annual back-to-school bedlam with my customary enthusiasm. First to be launched was Eldest Son, heading for his initiation into college life.

"I'll bet you'll really miss me, Mom," he mused one day as we stuffed a half-ton of denim into a twelve-by-twenty-four-inch duffel bag.

"I sure will," I told him, trying to keep a straight face. "How will I get through my evenings without the constant ringing of your phone, the pound-pound-pound of your CD player?"

"All right if I pack the microwave and the blender?"

"... the thrill of finding my gas gauge on E when I haven't driven in a week ..."

"I think I'll toss Dad's easy chair into the backseat of the car too."

"... the excitement of guessing will he/won't he eat

the entire pot roast before the rest of the family gets to the dinner table—"

"Hey, Ma, you aren't listening. I asked if you're going to miss me."

I gazed upward at my six-foot firstborn. Hadn't I hugged his tiny blanket-wrapped warmth close to me just a year or two ago? "Yes, dear," I said softly, ignoring a lump that had suddenly grown in my throat. "I am definitely going to miss you."

Next on the agenda was the high school pair. I waded through permit forms for golf team, debate team and steeple-chase team, and checked schedules.

"You didn't tell me you enrolled in both Advanced Lunch *and* Intermediate Study Hall," I admonished the junior. "Isn't that a bit heavy?"

"Funny, Ma. At least it keeps us enriched and out of your bathroom."

"Ah, yes," I sighed. "No more wet bathing suits on the coffee table. No more tennis racquets in the laundry chute, or midnight raids on the refrigerator with no milk left for your father's Sugartweets. How will I survive?"

"You'll think of a way."

I stared at the two of them. How had they gotten so tall just since last night? "Yes," I said, ignoring a strange soreness somewhere around my heart. "I'll think of a way."

The grade school pair, as usual, were the most challeng-ing. Would they/wouldn't they get Mrs. Allegra for chorus this year? Should they/shouldn't they take their giant-sized boxes of crayons to school on the first day, since one of the fifth-grade boys was sure to eat the red one—and maybe even the violet? Should they/shouldn't they attempt to smuggle a gerbil into the classroom or perhaps the iguana that Elder Brother had thoughtfully brought back from a trip to Florida?

"I don't know how you stand it," Spouse confided. "All that bickering would drive me crazy."

"You are crazy," I reminded him. "And actually, it's not that horrible because there's light at the end of the tunnel. No more lemonade stands, hamster races in the kitchen, golf balls in the dishwasher ..."

"... Popsicles on the front seat of my car ..."

"... Just endless days to do all the things I've been meaning to catch up on for the past twenty years."

Husband gave me a hug. "Does this mean you're planning to sew the button on that 1998 Little League Coach sweater of mine?"

But I didn't have time to answer, because the children were ready to leave. One son, cleaner than he'd been all summer, bearing the unmistakable aura of emerging maturity despite the toast crumbs still on his cheeks. One daughter, socks not quite hiding the bandages on her knees, reminders of a summer made for exploring and running—and growing.

"So long, Mom," they chorused as, hitting each other with lunch sacks, they headed for the back door. "Have a good day."

"A very good day," I murmured as I watched them skip across the street to the school bus stop. And ignored the tear trickling down my cheek.

Enjoy the little things, for one day
you may look back and realize
they were the big things.

—ROBERT BRAULT

31 Voluntary Guidelines

I have never understood why a woman, perfectly normal in every other respect, would feel it her solemn duty to volunteer. Of course, society needs us, especially with so many women in the full-time work world. The nation would dissolve under a sea of murk if women were not Out There campaigning for cleaner air or more frequent trash pickup. Clubs and organizations would screech to a standstill if someone didn't raise funds, prepare mailings and locate a decent caterer that specialized in fat-free menus. And how would the schools function with no lunchroom supervisors or Great Books leaders?

Yes, we're irreplaceable. And yet a woman should definitely think twice (nay, six times) before raising her hand and shrieking, "I'll do it!" There's nothing wrong—and a good deal right—about donating one's time and effort to a cause. But one must be cautious when deciding, for volunteering has an unwritten rule: If there's one place where you absolutely don't fit, that's the job you'll be assigned to do.

For example, as you know by now, I am known as Rachael Ray's alter ego. I loathe cooking. The very sight of a toaster can throw me into cardiac arrest. My recipe file contains only dishes involving three ingredients or less. On desperate days I serve ketchup as a vegetable.

Given this, it was only natural I be assigned to the school's hot-lunch program last fall. Spending my volunteer days hiding in the bathroom and sponging chocolate milk off tables, kids and other volunteers, I learned well: One must choose a job that fits her talents.

It's also important to read the fine print on signup sheets, to know precisely what is involved before saying "I do." Like most moms, I was so wildly excited on the first day of school last year that I would have signed anything, even adoption papers. So when someone waved a sheet marked Fine Arts Committee under my nose, I gladly added my signature, assuming it was a petition asking for additional enrichment in the classroom. It wasn't 'til later that I discovered I had volunteered to give the children a monthly presentation on art. I, whose sole experience with painting involved some linen closet shelves, was to lecture on the old masters. Pleading temporary insanity didn't help; I was given a Raphael print and told to "go get 'em."

The first few sessions were only semidismal. After all, I have written books about angels, and one would assume I could hold a class's interest with tales of the heavenly host. I was able to muddle through by leaning on the instruction sheet: "Do not impose adult taste. Stimulate the senses. Let the children talk." (Gladly, gladly!) But when a bespectacled fourth-grade boy asked me for an explanation of the Renaissance period, and a pigtailed six-year-old wanted to know why, if I liked color so much, I was wearing a black suit,

I realized I was eminently unqualified to meet the challenge. Moral: Read before signing.

Any woman who majored in Oriental Philosophy quite naturally gravitates toward a volunteer job as a teacher's aide. But beware. Though it sounds innocent enough ("all you'll do is hold up flash cards and take the children to the bathroom"), certain duties may be deliberately unmentioned.

For instance, will you be expected to use only a roll of leftover crepe paper to whip up clever bulletin boards depicting the joy of proper teeth brushing? Will you be responsible for removing modeling clay from the hair of the entire kindergarten class? Will you have to thread projectors, feed and exercise the class boa constrictor or perform other unskilled labor for which you are eminently unsuited? It's a good idea to ask questions and proceed cautiously.

Also, a woman who gets carsick on the two-block ride to church while in an air-conditioned sedan should think twice before volunteering to chaperone a group of Girl Scouts to Roller-Coaster Heaven in a bus that lost its shock absorbers a decade ago. Unfortunately for everyone, especially those seated close to me, I forgot to think twice, or even once.

Be wary, too, when getting involved in an offspring's projects. I couldn't have been prouder when my son sold fifty-eight frozen pizzas for his school band's fund-raiser— until I discovered that the pizzas had to be delivered, across a twelve-block area, in eighty-degree weather. Son had forgotten that I possessed no car or little red wagon, but merely a bicycle basket that held either a small wallet or a bottle of sunscreen, but not both at the same time. It had also slipped his mind that our freezer is three inches too narrow to accommodate pizza boxes, even if they are rapidly turning to mush.

Fortunately, the neighbors ran an emergency taxi service, but the following year I contributed a check to the band instead.

Ask yourself if you honestly have the time. It all sounds so simple—just a few hours on the telephone delivering room mother messages, or an afternoon staffing a booth at the grade school Fun Fair (make sure it isn't the goldfish concession—mothers tend to get frantic if their offspring win certain games). Think ahead. The time adds up.

"Where are you going with those voter registration lists and our telephone book?" my husband asked me last month.

"To choir practice."

"I didn't know the choir was politically active."

"They're not. I'm looking up voter telephone numbers for the regular Republication organization."

"While you're practicing the 'Hallelujah Chorus'?"

"Well, the concert's next week."

"And you overextended yourself again." Husband shot me one of his withering when-is-she-going-to-learn? glances as I slunk away.

Actually, I was a bit rushed. It wasn't that I resented making six dozen oatmeal cookies for the Math Club picnic (due tomorrow and I think we're out of oatmeal) or the tea I'd promised to attend for the Save Our Beavers League, but coordinating those events with the two women's clubs talks I would be giving next week (one involving a plane trip somewhere) was going to be tricky. And how does one fake it through the "Hallelujah Chorus"?

The lessons to be learned here are critical. One must be cautious and discriminating, as well as generous, when taking on volunteer jobs. And yet, as I began by asking, why does a perfectly normal woman continue to volunteer?

Simple. How else can she meet some of the nicest people in the world, avoid her ironing for another day—and learn about the Renaissance at the same time?

Next year I'm choosing Van Gogh.

A hundred years from now, it will not matter
what my bank account was, the sort of house I lived in,
or the kind of car I drove. But the world may be different,
because I was important in the life of a child.

—DR. FOREST E. WITCRAFT (1894–1967)

32 My Tattered Friend

"Oh, hi, Mrs. A," a shocked neighbor boy said as we met one day in the library. "I didn't recognize you!"

I wasn't surprised. The only time this child sees me is in the early morning when he stops by for my son on his way to school. And whatever the climate, the season or my disposition, I'm always wearing my faithful blue robe.

It's tattered, worn around the cuffs, stained with spit-up and baby juice. There's a gash in the floor-length hem, made when I leaped three stairs trying to head off the toddler, who had escaped from his crib.

But it's warm and comforting, too, like the hug of a good friend. As I drag my protesting body out of bed every morning, my robe wraps me in a blue cocoon, shielding me from the noise and confusion that accompanies each new day. For a little while, at least until my fuzzy mind adjusts, it is my buffer zone, my transition into sanity, my safe haven in the midst of the morning storm.

Friends would be aghast if they saw my ragged costume. (I've never been a neighborhood fashion trendsetter, but one should have some pride.) The garbagemen are definitely aghast. They identify me as "You know, the middle house, the one with the blue robe."

Even my usually understanding husband is not amused. "Maybe we should throw a benefit for you," he said yesterday, eying the stitches coming loose on my sleeve. "Or you could break down and *buy* a new robe."

But I shake my head. Like ancient treasure, my robe's value cannot be measured by surface charm. Each stain, each snag is a reminder of the past, evidence that in spite of the challenges of breakfast hour, I have managed to survive. My robe is my warm armor, my defense against the onslaught of spilled milk, toast crumbs and a multitude of lunch boxes— no two having the same contents—waiting to be packed. It is the comforting reassurance that future mornings can also be faced, if not happily, at least pleasantly. Despite endless traumas, I am fighting the good fight, I am running the race.

Actually, I suspect that my fixation on this obsolete garment has a hidden meaning. Could the robe possibly be what psychologists euphemistically refer to as a "lovey," an object of reassurance and contentment? True, loveys are usually limited to babies and small children who carry them everywhere while cuddling, rubbing or stroking them. But I'm not the only member of the family to cling to a useless scrap of fabric. What about our eldest who insists on using a specific yellow towel after showering ("... and I'll kill the first guy who grabs it")? Is he sentimental, picky or simply aware on some deeper level that years ago, we outfitted his crib with cuddly yellow bedding? Perhaps Mr. Macho seeks to resurrect that early feeling of comfort and security and has found the perfect substitute.

And what about my spouse? "Isn't it time you tossed your high school letter sweater, the one that's shrunk to size-four toddler?" I ask occasionally, while completing my annual dusting.

He usually drops the TV remote control in horror. "I may need that someday!"

"Are you planning to lose fifty pounds?" I continue relentlessly. "Besides, it's missing a sleeve."

"No way," he counters in a tone that says it's futile to argue.

So I don't. Because I understand, better than he thinks. I, too, have a lovey. And when the breakfast stampede has ended and I wave good-bye to the clan, my lovey's usefulness comes to a temporary end. For a while it will hang, hidden and shabby, in a corner of my closet, forgotten as I make my daily rounds in more acceptable garb, waiting patiently for its next summons. It has no doubts about tomorrow. And neither do I. Together, like two faithful friends, my robe and I will meet the dawn.

When I awake, let me be filled with your presence.

—PSALM 17:15 (NAB)

33 Neither Sleet nor Snow

I was reading an article on helping your child handle money when I realized that our children didn't have any money. Well, they have allowances but there isn't much there to handle. Besides, they would never ask for nor welcome any help in that area. I think their goal is to get the money away from my influence as soon as possible.

(We give the children part of the family income simply because they're part of the family and share in the needs as well as the benefits of family life. We don't take allowances away from them if they refuse to share in these needs, which they often try to do. That creates another strategy, but I'm getting off the subject.)

Our gang needed part-time jobs, I concluded. Something a little more challenging than lemonade stands but not quite as entrepreneurial as boarding canaries or making and selling fudge brownies. In short, they needed something that didn't involve me at all until it was time to "help child handle money."

That's when we entered the world of discarded twine, large metal rings with cardboard tags attached and pre-dawn telephone communication. What better job is available to a youngster than the hallowed profession of newspaper carrier?

In our area, the large metropolitan dailies are home-delivered by grim-looking adults who fire the papers out of speeding cars without a backward glance. Youngsters, there-fore, are left with their choice of weekly circulars or the small local daily paper.

"Seems like a good idea," Husband said one evening after I'd given the kids my you-are-going-to-love-being-a-productive-member-of-society pep talk. "Paper routes will teach them to be responsible and to set their own alarm clocks."

"And hopefully not to involve me in any way until they get paid," I added with typical helpfulness.

"Of course." Husband sighed wistfully, and I sensed a bit of nostalgia coming on. "Did I ever tell you about my first newspaper route? Trudging through the snow by the dawn's early light—"

"Yes, you did," I assured him quickly.

Number Three Child promptly decided to take on the Wednesday afternoon advertising circular. It was an after-school activity in the healthy outdoors, and there was no record-keeping involved because every house received a paper. What could be simpler and need less involvement from me? It wasn't until Son read the instruction sheet on that first Wednesday (okay, so I was glancing over his shoulder) that we discovered that the 125 circulars just delivered to our drive-way had to be personally rubber-banded to each doorknob on the route, rather than casually tossed against fence posts or steps or into trees. It was also against the law to put such paper into mailboxes. "Routes will be checked," the form warned ominously. Really. Were scare tactics needed? I remembered my noninvolvement pledge just as I was about to make an indignant phone call and instead cleaned the bathroom.

Son bravely loaded his bag (almost as tall as he) with half the route and set out on his appointed rounds. (Was it my imagination or were his little knees actually buckling under the strain?) By dinnertime, he had returned. "Only sixty-five more papers, Mom."

Was that thunder in the distance? Well, I could be non-involved *next* Wednesday. I left the older boys in charge of the roast beef, hauled the baby buggy out of the garage, buried Little Sister in the bottom and lovingly covered her with newspapers. Third Son took another bagful, and together we doorknobbed. By the time Baby's face was visible, the route was almost complete. Just three hours from beginning to end—and not an edible piece of meat left for dinner. "You just said to watch the roast," Eldest pointed out. "You didn't say to turn it off."

Our two older kids disdained this easy route in favor of the daily morning newspaper, bigger papers but much fewer. They began their jobs in late November, just in time for the tornado and/or blizzard season, each hauling a wagon/sled load of papers for blocks to the first house. Morning became intriguing as, from the comforts of my noninvolved bed, I eavesdropped on phone calls to the agency office ("I'm short a paper—drop it at the Jones' house") and marveled at the kids' growing efficiency.

Occasionally Husband would arise and cheerfully lend a hand. "Reminds me of my boyhood," he would inform all and sundry as they rolled, rubber-banded and checked vacation stops. "Did I ever tell you about my first newspaper route? Trudging through the snow——"

"Yep," the kids chorused.

Collection week was also a learning experience. Money had to be wrested from customers and then converted into a check to pay the news agency bill. The remainder went into the pockets of the carriers. I was always graciously allowed to take possession of twenty pounds of coins (many customers enjoyed paying with pennies) in exchange for the agency check, but everyone avoided asking me for help in "handling their money."

"We know you don't want to get involved, Mom."

"Yes, but I was going to explain the principle of compound interest to you . . ."

It wasn't working, I finally admitted. But something else was starting to happen. The kids were actually getting up on time, by themselves. Responsibility was maturing them in some indefinable but wonderful way; dealing with a variety of customers was giving them a richly varied perspective on life. And hadn't I just run into an elderly lady at church who complimented me on my thoughtful son, the one who always places the paper right near her door? Maybe there was more to learning and growing than "handling money" after all.

Through years of being the newsboys' mother, I have learned much about human nature—some of it disappointing, some positively uplifting. I have learned that newspaper subscribers often take good service for granted, rarely compliment but do complain when things are less than perfect. I have learned that every route has its cheater—the customer who doesn't answer when the newsboy rings to collect his pay.

Then there are God's Beautiful People: the man who comes out in the freezing dawn to fix a small boy's broken sled strap, the elderly lady who warms the spirit with cocoa, the neighbor who clips a thank-you note to his mailbox. Starting one's day off with people like these can't help but encourage a cold and running-late carrier.

In our house, the paper business is likely to continue; just a few more years and it will be little Daughter's turn to shoulder that familiar gray bag. In fact . . .

"Daddy?" she asked yesterday. "Were you ever a paper delivery person?"

Husband lowered the paper warily. "Didn't I ever tell you about my first route? Trudging through the alley by the dawn's early light?"

"No." She grabbed her blanket, stuck her thumb in her mouth and climbed comfortably into his lap. "Tell me."

Each day of our lives we make deposits
in the memory banks of our children.

—CHARLES R. SWINDOLL
THE STRONG FAMILY

34 Ah, Those Memories

C an it be possible?" began the letter. "Is it time for us to get going on another class reunion?"

I was thrilled. It's always a puzzle to me why some people groan when a class reunion invitation appears in their e-mail or mailbox. Or perhaps our old grade school group is unique in our desire to stay in touch with those who shared such an important part of our childhoods. Our reunions occur not in an orderly pattern—we were always a somewhat disorganized bunch—but whenever the committee feels like seeing one another again.

We committee people meet one night and divide into the same two groups: those who will handle the evening itself (catering, awards, music and the hide-and-seek competition) and the "Find-'Em-by-Phone" contingent (locating pals, sending invitations and collecting updates for the Minutes of the Meeting booklet sent to everyone after the event). Since I was born with a telephone grafted to my ear, I am part of the latter group.

"Guess what became of Michael O'Mara!" I tell Husband one night as I address invitations.

"Is it true? You're really throwing another reunion?" He sinks behind the sports section. Husband graduated from the same grade school a few classes ahead of me, but he's always been a bit thin in the auld lang syne department. (He tells our kids that this is because the teachers gave him extra credit whenever he was absent from class.)

"Come on," I urge. "You remember Michael, don't you?"

Husband sighs. "Wasn't he the loon that drove the ice cream truck down the center aisle in church one morning?"

"You're thinking of Martin Mulcahey. Michael set the convent kitchen on fire."

"Whatever. He's probably doing five to ten in a federal pen by now."

"Nope. He's our UN Ambassador to Samoa."

"It figures."

Our committee meets again to share the updated news and responses that our classmates have sent from across the universe. "I'll be bringing my Roy Rogers scrapbook," Fred assures us. "If I can reschedule my liposuction, I'll be there," Claudia pens. Sally wants to know if anyone else will be wearing penny loafers and a white felt skirt with poodle appliqués (she always was the class trendsetter), and since they are back in style, I reassure her that she'll fit right in. Counting reluctant spouses and an occasional retired nun, the reservations portend another overflow crowd. It seems safe to order that case of Green River for the true nostalgia buffs.

The night arrives, and I ignore Husband's stiff-upper-lip

expression as we begin our trip down Memory Lane. Actually, it starts in the old parish church where one of our favorite priests celebrates a prayer service with us. Father deftly turns down Michael O'Mara's offer to be an acolyte. Michael once set his cassock on fire. Claudia thinks it was during our Confirmation Mass when he attempted to light some incense, but as I told her, I have trouble remembering yesterday, much less my Confirmation. We then proceed to the blue-and-white festooned gymnasium where, yes, there are those familiar faces, grinning, everyone hugging, elbowing one another aside to view the memento table that displays relics of our past. Fred's scrapbook is there, I note, along with old report cards, photographs, the tardy bell. Two former fullbacks recall competing in their brown oxfords because neither could afford the regulation shoes.

Husband yawns. "Isn't it time for Pom-pom yet?"

"Not until we present the special award for the Couple-Married-the-Longest-and-Still-Speaking-to-Each-Other," I remind him. "You've got time to dance the Bunny Hop with Sister Beatrice. And don't forget to sign her autograph book."

By now the crowd is swapping memories, sharing stories and family photos, clicking cameras and feeding the firemen who put out the wastebasket blaze accidentally started by Michael O'Mara's cigar. Sally compliments me on my giant hair bow and I dutifully admire her felt skirt and cinch belt. My best friend wins the "Classmate-Who-Has-Changed-the-Least" award (a bottle of hair dye) and Claudine enthralls the admiring crowd with details of her liposuction. The "Classmate-Who-Came-the-Farthest" award (a yardstick) is presented to Tom from California who, overcome with emotion, sobs, "I came all the way from Anaheim and this is all I get?" The entire evening is our usual success.

Even Husband admits it's a success. As we walk toward the parking lot, sleepy but exhilarated, he comments, "I remember tacking pictures of Marilyn Monroe on the hall bulletin boards. Haven't thought of that in years. Funny how it all comes back."

"I'm amazed that the nuns let *you* back," I tell him. "And why doesn't your class ever sponsor a reunion?"

"*Sh*," he tells me. "Sister Beatrice and I are working on it. And guess what happened to Odette O'Malley?"

Ah, memories.

Joan's Reasons to Celebrate Maturity:

• No one cares if you spill your dinner on your pajamas.

• There's nothing left to learn the hard way.

• Things you buy now won't wear out.

35 The Undersigned Pledge To...

The other day I was reading a book on coping with teenagers, written by a psychologist who, the credits informed me, has two children, ages four and two. (This is akin to reading an article on managing one's home efficiently, written by a female CEO who employs a full-time secretary and maid.) Anyhow, the expert on adolescents suggested that instead of arguing over every petty conflict ("Mom, I'm getting married . . . buying a St. Bernard . . . hitchhiking to Alaska . . .") we parents should keep cool heads and instead negotiate a contract with our teens. We write everything up all nice and legal-like, and we are all bound by the terms. If we break our promises, the kids don't have to keep theirs, and vice versa.

I have to admit, I was intrigued. The idea of sitting down with our teens and having a *conversation* was exciting enough, much less attempting a series of high-level negotiations prior to writing up a document and, I presume, having it notarized. But I was tired of one-word sentences passing for intimate revelations and was willing to try anything. And if we had all agreements typed in a large black font, maybe my husband wouldn't have to spend his weekends shouting, "You did what?" to everyone over the age of twelve.

The psychologist had suggested we begin with a not-so-important-but-only-mildly-irritating issue before tackling a major problem, thus giving us a chance to perfect our communication skills. I decided to hold our first meeting on the subject of walking the dog. Assembling the crowd, I gaveled for silence (actually, no one was talking) and began.

"As you know, when we got Snooky, he was to be the sole responsibility of your eldest brother. However, Brother's away at college now, and Snooky hasn't had a proper walk in ages. Who would like to take over the task?"

Blank stares greeted me.

"Take those iPods out of your ears and listen!" I shouted. "Who's going to walk the dog?"

"Why can't we keep tossing him out the back door and taking our chances?" asked Fifteen.

"Because it's the neighbors who are taking the chances," I explained, "and some of them are getting justifiably testy. Don't you understand? I'm trying to negotiate a contract with you. One of you will walk Snooky and in return, you'll earn a privilege."

Light dawned. "You mean you'll *give* me something if I walk the dog?" asked Fifteen.

"I'll give you a privilege," I said, referring quickly to the book.

"How about letting me drive a new BMW, complete with stereo, whitewalls—"

"We don't own a BMW."

"But we could buy one."

"Not unless all of you want to give up eating for the next several years," Husband pointed out.

"And besides, you don't have a license," his brother added.

"And we're not negotiating driving at the moment," I said desperately. "That's a *hard* issue. We're practicing on something simple."

The blank stares were back. Little Sister sidled up to me, a sweet smile on her face. "I'll walk Snooky, Mommy," she purred, "if you let me have a Chinese hamster."

"But—"

"Sold!" Husband reached for a piece of paper. "Write it up, Dear. If Daughter forgets to walk the dog, we bring her hamster back to the pet store. Say, this contract business is great!"

Husband might have been impressed, but he wasn't doing the negotiating, at least not yet. His acid test came the following weekend when he drove into the garage and ran over two paint cans (full), a bicycle basket (empty) and his beloved electric drill that had been missing since last summer. "I've called you here together," he droned at the crowd, "to work out a compromise on the matter of the garage. Here are my terms. No one under voting age will be allowed to enter it under any circumstances."

"What will you give us if we honor your terms?" asked Fifteen (he was catching on fast).

"In return for your cooperation, you will be allowed to live in our home and partake of services such as heat, electricity, running water and meals."

"You've got a real heart, Dad. What if we renege?"

"If you're that fond of the garage, your bed will be moved there."

Silence. "Not much of a deal," Fifteen muttered. "Of course I *could* sleep in a BMW."

Husband quickly typed up the document, enlarged the font and got it signed during a commercial. I had to admire his aplomb. "We're rolling now," he told me. "What's next on the negotiations agenda?"

"Big ticket items," I warned him. "Driving, curfews, use of the house phone, job hours, dating rules, money handling."

"All that? Why don't I just flex my muscles and shout?"

I sighed. "Because we're trying to give the teens some control over their lives, to teach them to accept responsibilities as well as consequences, to make mature decisions—" I stopped as Fifteen handed me a legal-looking paper. It read:

"We the undersigned, being of sound minds, do hereby agree to keep our rooms tidy IF:

(1) Mom quits playing the piano.

(2) Dad loses fifteen pounds this year and dumps that old plaid sport coat."

We stared at each other. "But I like that sport coat," Husband murmured.

"Start shouting," I told him, "while I go and set fire to a certain book."

Grown-ups never understand anything for themselves,
and it is tiresome for children to be always and
forever explaining things to them.

—Antoine de Saint-Exupéry
The Little Prince

36 Happy ~~39th~~ (Sort Of)

I've turned thirty-nine on several occasions, and I get more professional each time I celebrate. I love being this age (or a reasonable facsimile thereof). It's the time of life when, as my best friend put it, your insides finally match your outsides. The youthful "if onlys" and "when I grow ups" have given way to the philosophy of one day at a time. A thirty-nine-year-old (give or take a few inches) is not old enough to live with only memories as companions; she is still surrounded by family, laundry, bills, a constantly ringing telephone, classes and probably a job—monuments to her midlife. Demands are constant and the pace is a whirlwind, but she is learning to wring the best from each moment.

There's no need to pretend either. All those years when I tiptoed around a subject, worried about other people's sensitive psyches—either that approach got to be too difficult or I simply outgrew it. Our children, for example, will never have to pay a shrink one hundred dollars an hour to find out why I rejected them. Now I tell them why I'm rejecting them—because they eat all the chocolate doughnuts I hide in the piano bench or never clean their rooms or don't bother to remove Mommy's nighties from the washing machine when they launder their mud-encrusted orange soccer uniforms.

Even though I still rejoice in awe and gratitude when Husband makes the coffee, at this point in our relationship, we both know it's merely an act. However, men do need positive feedback when they attempt to master a growing number of domestic duties.

And it's a price I'm prepared to pay.

There are women, of course, who don't share my philosophy. One neighbor recently celebrated her fortieth birthday by locking herself in her room and weeping all afternoon. I honestly didn't understand it. Being forty isn't so bad. It certainly doesn't mean she's over the hill; she's just on the edge and has to hang on a little harder.

Of course there are some drawbacks to aging. For one, it takes longer to look good. The days are long gone when I could roll out of bed, run a comb through my hair and confidently greet the morning. Now my laugh lines have turned to wrinkles, I'm never without my beloved cover-up stick, I need bifocals to read newspaper headlines and I find myself listening avidly to those Botox and liposuction commercials. Just to keep informed, of course.

Then too, everyone around me seems to be getting younger. Our new associate pastor, for example, is still in a retainer brace and my internist wears a class sweater while drawing blood. And when Husband's eyes glazed over recently at the sight of the newest Miss America, I casually reminded him that she's the same age as our eldest. It's a dirty job—and I hate to see a grown man cry—but someone has to do it.

The real problem with being thirty-nine (or thereabouts) is not really mine or yours; it's the way society views getting older. Some techniques, however, can make this trip a little easier. Consider the following:

1. Don't tell anyone how old you actually *are*. Your mother and your bridge club will know, but why should they blow their own cover? Your husband will probably forget; a man who can't remember where (or why) he parked the car at the mall last week and had to wait until it closed and everyone left before he found it may be fooled forever. Your kids, of course, consider anyone over voting age a candidate for dementia, but when have they ever been encouraging and supportive except when asking for money?

2. Avoid conversations revolving around body parts. Never complain about arthritis, bridgework, calcium deficiencies, slipped discs, the price of a root canal or other conditions associated with falling apart. Especially do not complain about how hot it is in here.

3. Stay in shape. If you can't bear the idea, then get in the habit of wearing sweats and carrying a tennis racket when you make your appointed rounds. If you can be a bit breathless, so much the better.

4. Volunteer for positions such as Cub Scout den mother, band chaperone or hockey scorekeeper. Act enthusiastic about attending school conferences, track meets and fun fairs. Remember, the older a mother is, the longer it takes her to work up enthusiasm for the above-named activities.

5. When entertaining, hide wrinkle cream, hormone supplements and other stay-young products under your bed. Give guests

who might snoop through your medicine cabinet something to think about by placing only lip gloss, blush and acne medication on a prominent shelf.

6. Refrain from publicly humming any song more than two years old. Bone up on modern melodies and movie titles—even though you wouldn't spend a dime for any currently out. Instead of conversing normally, learn to shriek and/or giggle when anyone asks you a question.

Finally, have a wonderful thirty-ninth (or thereabouts) birthday party. And trust me—they'll get better every year.

> Grow old along with me, the best is yet to be.
> The last of life, for which the first was made.

> —ROBERT BROWNING (1812–1889)

37 One Way to Get a Gumdrop

I will never forget (although God knows I've tried) the various ways our children have celebrated Halloween. It's hard to believe that in the early years, I actually encouraged them. Our Volume One photo album chronicles the procedures involved in getting two tots dressed for the big house-to-house tour. The older one is wearing a red cap, red leotards borrowed from my bridge partner (the mother of girls) and his red sweater. Attached to the sweater is the imaginative sign "I'm a little devil." The younger one wears a white pillowcase, a tinfoil halo and the sign "I'm a little angel" (and he definitely was until he learned to walk, which is an entirely different story).

The camera also records the disintegration of the entire event, starting from the first house where friendly Mrs. Murphy has turned into a witch (bringing on a chorus of startled screams), to the last house, where our angel starts to arm-wrestle his brother for a gumdrop (bringing on a chorus of angry screams).

I brought the pair home, put them down for naps (out-raged screams) threw away the dented halo, ate the gum-drops and vowed to avoid Halloween forever.

I was successful for a while. Over the next few years, our kids seemed perfectly happy to simply answer the doorbell and pass out candy. That is, until the eldest started preschool and, one day in mid-October, asked the fateful question: "What am I going to be for Halloween?"

I thought fast. He had outgrown his red sweater and the pillowcase had made an excellent dust rag. "How about a farmer?" I suggested brightly, thinking of his jeans in the closet. "Or a cowboy?" He owned a plaid shirt too.

Son shook his head. "I want to be the Tin Man."

"The Tin—?"

"Like in *The Wizard of Oz.*"

Since he was our first child and we hadn't yet discovered the phrase "Over my dead body," Husband and I actually made him a Tin Man costume. The cost of the aluminum foil alone equaled our weekly food budget—to say nothing of the hours spent cutting and stapling. "What happened to the good old days?" asked my rapidly aging spouse. "Didn't we dress up as firemen and clowns?"

"True. But look on the bright side. The other kids can wear this costume too."

And they could have, if Eldest hadn't madly wrestled a classmate for a gumdrop, which led to the complete destruc-tion of our investment in aluminum foil and our enthusiasm for Halloween.

Our offspring, however, continued to embrace it eagerly. During the next several years they dressed in store-bought outfits: Darth Vader, Barney and sundry skeletons. They hosted parties and attended them. One year they made several life-sized dummies, posed them in various stages of mayhem on a neighbor's roof, and accompanied the scene with amplified recordings of moans, groans, screams and howls. It was a traffic-stopper. Fortunately the neighbor was having her appendix out that day, and her children considerately spared her the details.

On other Halloweens, our brood cut up our best king-sized sheets for ghost costumes, used my cosmetics and paint for makeup (Note: Turpentine does not necessarily remove paint from a child's face, although it does remove skin), and put toilet paper in the trees of our favorite—and now former —friends. The weather also contributed to our holiday memories. The year of the blizzard, for example. The kids' trick-or-treating was limited to the house next door, lest a pint-sized E.T. get lost in a drift. Soon we learned to buy costumes that fit over snowsuits.

As our traditions evolved, I began to feel vaguely uncomfortable letting our brood take part in what I had come to realize was a pagan holiday. But I fell back on Anderson's theory of relativity: "Is this going to matter in ten years? If so, dig in your heels and stand firm. If not, take a nap." I also spent a lot of Halloweens staying up late to sneak through their pumpkin bags at midnight, removing all the gumdrops for my own sweet tooth.

Then came that day one October when our youngest son posed the inevitable rite-of-passage question: "Mom and Dad, when is someone too old to go trick-or-treating?"

His father and I discussed it. "When you drive yourself

from house to house? When you can't eat any of the candy, because your dentures are slipping? When people answer the door in their pajamas? When your beard catches in your mask?"

Son grinned. "I know it's kid stuff, yet . . ."

Yet there was a part of him that couldn't let go. I remembered the "I'm a little devil" sign, the Tin Man costume, the dummies, bathroom tissue, makeup and fun, and knew just how he felt.

"There's always the costume contest judging downtown," I pointed out. "And didn't I hear something about the middle school sponsoring a haunted house tour?"

He brightened. "Hey, yeah. And I guess just ringing a few doorbells wouldn't hurt, would it?"

"Not if you bring home some gumdrops," his father agreed.

After all, our youngest just saw *The Wizard of Oz* for the first time.

Backward, turn backward,
O Time, in your flight
Make me a child again
just for tonight!

—ELIZABETH AKERS ALLEN (1832–1911)
"ROCK ME TO SLEEP, MOTHER"

38 Give Thanks for Thanksgiving

Thanksgiving at our house usually starts right after the Halloween candy has been eaten. Small Daughter takes down the black-cat cutouts that have decorated our picture window and replaces them with her hand-crayoned version of Mr. Gobbler. The bird and I are now destined to exchange beady glances for the next three weeks, but he's probably a fortunate reminder—I need three weeks to get ready for Thanksgiving.

As many of you know by now, I do not entertain gracefully. In fact, given an option, I probably would not entertain at all except that it seems the most practical way to enjoy the company of those I love. I don't know why I find it difficult to talk and stir a pot of beans at the same time—I come from a long line of gracious and welcoming hostesses—but one must accept one's limitations and carry on. And so, because I have the largest house and the loudest family, the holiday parties frequently fall on my shoulders.

The first item on my agenda is figuring out how many people will share the turkey, hence, how many tables, napkins, saltshakers and cornucopia centerpieces will be required. Determining this tally can create some new age lines since our clan tends to be casual about making plans. Will my Minneapolis-based sister and her clan make the trip? ("If the airlines aren't on strike and the cat has her kittens on her due date, we'll be there, I promise!") Will my Eldest bring a date to share the bounty? (And will she, poor girl, be a political liberal in a houseful of conservatives and have to dine in a closet in order to preserve peace?) Will my brother and his gang share supper with the in-laws and arrive here only for dessert? (Set up crib for baby niece?) And will my college son surprise me with a roommate or two? ("This is Al, Mom. He'll sleep anywhere, and he's real good at peeling potatoes.") (Put Al in crib?) The only constant in this crisis is my husband's side of the extended family; since there are so many of them, we get together only for outdoor affairs, so none will be attending our banquet. But perhaps some of the cousins will drop in later. Extra peanuts? Extra soda?

Having assembled a loose guest list, I now turn to household preparations. Or rather, my spouse does. "Maybe I ought to paint the kitchen before Christmas," he muses.

"Paint the kitchen? Why?"

"Because it's there," he says philosophically. "And also because it needs it."

"It's needed painting for the past year," I protest. "Why now? Do we want oil fumes mingling with the turkey aroma?"

"It'll only take a day or two. And then you can clean out all the cabinets and arrange the canned goods in alphabetical order."

Husband has a peculiar sense of timing; he once shortened a table leg with his electric saw as the guests were arriving, sending a shower of sawdust into the yogurt dip. But because he's adept at scrubbing dirty bathtubs and organizing children's work details, I agree. Might as well take advantage of such a willing mate. (And actually, the kitchen's needed painting for *two* years.)

The rest of the household doesn't fare as well. "Why do I hafta clean my bedroom?" Fourth Grader argues. "I cleaned it last year, for Pete's sake. And no one will be upstairs anyway."

"Grandma will want to see your new wallpaper," I point out. "And you can never tell who'll decide to take a breather from the political arguments and eat dinner on the stairs."

"Can't I just close the door and hang a 'Quarantine—Sick Gerbils' sign on it?"

"Clean the room. Now."

If one could just prepare for the holidays, life would be simple indeed. But of course, other obligations intrude. The clan needs ongoing laundry, meals, chauffeuring services. I'm due at choir practice for our Thanksgiving church service. (My choir robe also needs to be ironed, and since I sold the ironing board at last summer's garage sale, this will be interesting.) Fourth Grader is leaving for a Boy Scout campout and cannot locate his mess kit, duffel bag or uniform. Small Daughter mentions casually that she has been exposed to a pal's "step throat." I'm supposed to have four chapters of my current book manuscript to the publisher by November twentieth, but haven't started writing them yet. And in a fit of vacuuming, Husband dislodges the freezer coils. "That'll be $150, ma'am. Sorry I couldn't get here any sooner, but you'll figure out what to do with all that thawed ground beef."

As the Big Event moves closer, it's finally time to Shop for Groceries. Now, of course, with a large family, one visits the supermarket at eight-hour intervals and is on a first-name basis with the produce manager and most of the teenage baggers. But Shopping for Groceries takes on major significance when a holiday meal is involved. No tripping blithely down the aisles, tossing bathroom tissue in the cart because it seems like a good idea, or trying to remember if one is out of mayonnaise. No, for Thanksgiving the kitchen is inventoried (at least it's in alphabetical order now), recipes perused and a list made of every single ingredient down to the dash of paprika for the mashed potatoes. I refuse to get involved as the youngest two slyly visit the meat counter and pop holes in the ground beef packages. I don't want the butcher to know what kind of savages I'm raising. (Why *do* they enjoy this activity so much?)

Our college son has arrived home by a circuitous route. ("Dad, the guys are going to drop me and Al off at the intersection of Route 42 and Grand Avenue; don't panic if we're not there till ten—Bud's car has been making a funny noise.") Son has proceeded to trail shoes, jackets, duffel bags and Al throughout the house, necessitating another round of vacuuming. "Who ate all the stale bread for the stuffing?"

I shriek the night before Thanksgiving. "Will someone get that iguana off the couch? Did anyone remember to buy groceries for the Food Pantry collection tomorrow at church?"

Silence. (And my choir robe still isn't ironed.) But thank heavens for Al—he does wield a mean potato peeler.

Thanksgiving dawns briskly, producing a light dusting of snow and a thin but steady stream of sunshine. I have wrestled the turkey into the oven, the coffee is perking and soon we will all be at church, starting the holiday where the best days always begin, with God. I will stand in the choir loft, skin prickly as we move into the strains of "Battle Hymn of the Republic" and look down on the heads of my family. *I love them so much, Father. Thank You. And please don't let the bean casserole burn.*

Home again to a massive breakfast and a massive cleanup job, which Al tackles with zest. (I wonder if he'd let me adopt him.) A fuse has blown and our engineering student locates the trouble and fixes it calmly. *Funny how the rewards of parenthood pop up in the oddest places.*

And here comes our extended family. Hugs, kisses. "It's so good to see you" and "Remind me to tell you . . ." The little folk dash upstairs, chattering happily, to break out the latest video game, and the rest of us gather in our too-small kitchen, eating spinach blobs, exchanging news and remarking "My, how you've grown!" to any youth who wanders in. (This is a stock comment for our college student who, indeed, grows an inch every month.) My mother checks the turkey. "Just perfect," she pronounces, "and your orange Jell-O mold looks lovely." *She always could find the positive aspects in whatever*

I did; what a wonderful world it would be if everyone had a mother like her.

I pass hors d'oeuvres and take stock. Eldest's date is holding her own quite nicely in an argument with Uncle Harry over socialized medicine; my sisters are singing harmony in the corner with an occasional assist from one of the neighbors who stopped by with an extra box of peanut brittle and stayed to join the chorus. Three of the teens are debating my brother-in-law over the merits (or demerits) of the Chicago Cubs, a small child is screaming upstairs and Mom is basting the turkey. All normal. *All so wonderfully normal. Are all families like this? If not, God, why not?*

My husband, flushed from an arm-wrestling victory with Nephew, flashes me the high sign—it's turkey time. Are the casseroles done? Potatoes mashed? Knife sharpened? We crowd around the Master Carver as he gives each of us a tantalizing nibble. Eldest Son is stirring gravy, Fourth Grader lighting candles, Al washing the little ones' hands (why *can't* I keep him?), and my sister's carrying hot dishes to the table. *Father, it all looks good, smells good—I think we've done it!*

And now the time of unity. Heads bowed, we give thanks for this day and for all the days that have led to it. All the moments, infinitely precious, the choices, the decisions that have bound us together as a family. All the memories to hold closely in our hearts, now and forever. Amen.

"The turkey looks great, hon." Spouse gives me one of those special smiles.

"Don't like gravy," protests Baby Niece.

"And so I said to Pastor O'Brien . . ."

"Socialism. That's what it is—just plain socialism."

"Please pass the orange stuff there."

"It's been on the best-seller list for over six months."

"Grandpa, how come your hair's gray?"

"Okay, so what about the White Sox?"

"And you'll never guess what the professor said."

"It's probably just a stage she's going through."

"Please pass that green stuff there."

It's a perfect Thanksgiving, God. Thank You so much, for everything

> Now thank we all our God, with hearts and hands and voices
> Who wondrous things hath done, in whom this world rejoices.
>
> —MARTIN RINKHART (1586–1649)

39 What Is December?

It's the last month of the year, but you shouldn't try ending anything in December. It's not the time to bring the upstairs bathroom project to a close just because extra people will be using it and will notice that you ran out of wallpaper behind the door and haven't stained the woodwork. Nor should you attempt to complete your afghan project for Aunt Lily, since in the intervening months (years) you have completely forgotten how to crochet. Planning to do anything in December, other than survive, is expecting too much of yourself. It's that kind of month.

One of the major December duties that you *must* do is pick out your Christmas cards (if you didn't buy them on sale last December twenty-sixth). After purchasing them, you inspect your mailing list to prune a name or two in the interest of economy and orderliness. After all, is there any good reason to send a greeting to the waitress at the budget pizza parlor where you and your husband would sometimes go when escaping the preschoolers? Or to your one-time babysitter who now has children of her own? Or to the plastic surgeon who did such a nice job on Child Number Four's broken nose? Be aware, of course, that as soon as you remove Sally and Kyle—folks from the old neighborhood whom you haven't heard from since 1999—you'll receive a card from them. In fact, other than the season's greetings from the dry cleaner, it will be the first card to arrive, with one of those jolly newsletters inside. You know the type: "Kyle, the kids and I spent a month on the yacht enjoying our annual cruise. This year we went to the Bahamas where Tammy was spotted by a TV producer; look for her in an upcoming episode of *How I Met Your Mother*. I passed the bar and was sent to Washington, DC (again!) for a major law conference . . ."

It would be hard to compete with that update; in fact the recipients of your letter will be yielding to terminal yawns before the second paragraph: "We had our usual year: Mom won an Honorable Mention at the annual Pot Holder Festival; Dad pursued his hobbies of napping and doing crosswords; Jimmy learned to cross the street alone. . . ." Forget it. Instead, make a donation to a favorite charity with your stamp money.

During December you'll spend a lot of time shopping. On the surface, it seems wise to purchase Christmas gifts well in advance, but then you have the problem of hiding them until the big day. There is not much room in the average-sized domicile to conceal a new tricycle or dollhouse. (Behind the jackets? Under the waffle iron?) Smaller items present a different challenge.

"What happened to the new chess set?" Husband asked me last week.

"We hid it so the kids couldn't find it," I reminded him.

"Well, where did we hide it?"

"I don't know. The kids haven't found it."

Prepare to ride many escalators and stand in endless lines to confer with Santa (these are the reasons you have not finished the bathroom wallpaper), but try to keep your perspective. For example, if you spot a pair of plain pink boots in size twelve that your daughter has been hoping for, don't go to five other stores to inspect their selection of plain pink boots. They won't be plainer or pinker, and even if they're slightly cheaper, they'll only be available in size eleven, so that eventually Daughter will develop ingrown toenails and complain loudly when you're in a crowd. A penny saved is not always a wise idea, especially in December.

December also demands some sort of holiday décor. If your first floor usually resembles a bus station waiting room, and your family has never realized that the ironing board folds up, decorating may be more of a challenge. You can always start by thumbtacking Sally and Jim's card to a door frame and laying an evergreen branch on the dining room table, but first remove school books, coats, gym shorts, clarinet, calorie counter, Scout badges, teddy bear and dust. If you are terribly ambitious, you can make one of those gumdrop castle centerpieces instead. Then you will have to throw several parties so that guests can view the castle and say things like, "You made this? You really did? Aren't you amazing?" You're the only one who can decide if the tradeoff is worth it.

List-making reaches its peak during December. You should probably post a chore chart on the refrigerator, of course, to help perpetuate the myth that you have everything under control: "Clean your rooms, including under beds, by the twenty-fourth. This means YOU!!!!" But most of your random jottings are indecipherable: "Raisins, batteries, red skirt, basketball hoop; mail Jay, Audrey, David, Bernadette, Tommy; sub/playground duty; cough syrup, cold tablets, aspirin, ear drops, call pediatrician; order turkey. Don't lose this list!"

The year I searched high and low for a broccoli cookie recipe, I finally realized that December can only be fully appreciated if one forgets about dieting. Personally, I envy Santa; he gets to wear the same outfit to one holiday party after another, and no one expects him to stay svelte. I'm not suggesting that we go—you'll excuse the expression—hog wild, but sprinkling cottage cheese with green sparkles or making a punch out of tomato juice seems to carry things a bit far. You can either pay attention to calories during December, or have a lot of fun during December, but you can't do both. I suggest the fun.

December is tinsel and holly and candles, candy canes and stars on a cold clear night, the smell of balsam and cinnamon, the taste of postage stamps and snowflakes. It's "Who took the cellophane tape?" and "What did Baby Jesus look like?" It's glory, tired feet, shining eyes and love. It's going-home time, it's making-memories time . . . and best of all, it comes every year.

It comes every year and will go on forever. And along with
Christmas belong the keepsakes and the customs.
Those humble, everyday things a mother clings to and ponders,
like Mary in the secret spaces of her heart.

—Marjorie Holmes (1910–2002)

40 The Last Word

Dear Friends, Moms and Grandmoms,

Thank you for hanging in there throughout these chapters. I'm hoping that you found some solace here and perhaps a laugh or two that lightened your spirit and helped you feel less alone. I hope you saw your own family reflected in mine—the good, the bad and the ugly—and realized that we all go through difficulties, loss and misunderstandings, and your problems are far more common than you knew. (And you're a nice person, too, despite it all.) Maybe you garnered a solution here or decided to try a new attitude in your wife-and-mothering rounds. Maybe you called a friend and suggested going out for lunch.

When you peek in to check your sleeping children tonight (or while you're pinching yourself awake waiting up for them to call, visit or just come home), I hope that, whatever their ages, this book has helped you to notice their positive qualities—the goodness that we so often take for granted in our quest to make everything perfect. Think for a moment of something dear and delightful that one of them said or did today, and bless that child in a special way. Tomorrow, try to remember it, especially if Child is not especially dear and delightful. Consider too that, if you live an average lifespan, there will be years to get out of debt, to organize the closets, to go on a cruise. But your children will be with you for only a small portion of their lives. See that they remember, more than anything, your love.

Finally, as mentioned, do not forget that God is your cocreator and is standing by, waiting to pull His share of the load. (Only the reckless would ignore His constant presence and affection.) Keep in mind that He knew your spouse and your child long before you did, and He has a plan for everyone in your family. Go to Him first, not as an afterthought when other solutions haven't worked. And teach your children to pray too.

That's about it, my friend. I must go and defrost something for dinner. So much for planning ahead. I guess some things never change.

Love,
Joan

A Note from the Editors

Guideposts, a nonprofit organization, touches millions of lives every day through products and services that inspire, encourage and uplift. Our magazines, books, prayer network and outreach programs help people connect their faith-filled values to their daily lives. To learn more, visit www.guideposts.com or www.guidepostsfoundation.org.